THE
SILVER HORN
OF
ROBIN HOOD

Gary Wells

Cover Illustration by
Kezzie Carey

Published by
Alaska Dreams Publishing
P.O. Box 72156
Fairbanks, Alaska 99707
www.alaskadp.com

ISBN-13: 978-0985558826
ISBN-10: 0985558822

First Alaska Dreams Publishing
Paperback printing May, 2012

E-Book version also available

DEDICATION

When I was a senior in high school I had an English teacher who believed in me when I could barely believe in myself.

It is with affectionate appreciation that I dedicate this book to Mrs. Estelene Bodenhamer.

CONTENTS

ACKNOWLEDGMENTS

The list of friends and family who have suffered through rough drafts, rewrites, and rejection slips would be a book of its own. But a handful do deserve special recognition:

Alan Corrick—his critical eye gave me direction without changing my voice.

Linda Huelskutter—our literary discussions at the break table was the genesis of much of my early efforts.

My daughters, Caitlin and Carly—for years they would laughingly challenge me to match their blue ribbon count, and rejoiced with every one I brought home.

My twin-brother-from-another-mother, Steve Olsen, he has walked with me down paths where it often seemed like we were the only ones. But deep down we knew we were not alone...

Because there is a God who weeps over the painful tragedies of man.

GARY WELLS

CHAPTER ONE

I was ten, soon to be eleven. School was out and it was going on summer. Clear skies with an occasional thunderstorm, warm evenings with lightning bugs, and Cubs games on the radio nearly every day; corn and soybeans in the fields, apples in the trees, and an occasional channel-cat down at Grampa's favorite fishing hole. There were weeds to pull in the garden, grass to mow in the yard, and sweet tea to drink in the early afternoon; that was summer in small town central Illinois in 1962.

For the first time that I could remember, my mother and I were living in the same house that we had been in the previous summer. Actually, the coming September would mark two years of being in the same house. All in all I can recollect seven different places that, up to that point in time, I had called home. The houses and apartments had all been on the same side of town, most of them within a few blocks of each other. Among other things, not moving meant I didn't have to learn new routes to the library, the movie theater, my school, and to my grandfather's house.

Back then, I measured distance by city blocks. It was two blocks to the little store where I cashed in soda bottles and bought comic books. It was three blocks to Jefferson Elementary School where I would be in the sixth grade come the day after Labor Day. It was seventeen blocks to the public library, twenty blocks to the Crown Motion Picture Theater, and an entire thirty-five blocks—clean to the other side of town—to Grampa's house. I seldom walked all the way to Grampa's.

Our house was an older two-bedroom cottage with a living room, a bathroom and a kitchen large enough to hold a small dining table. There were covered porches running the width of the house in front and back. The front porch had flower boxes along the edge facing the street and a couple of rocking chairs on one end with a small table between them. Mom and Grampa liked to sit on the porch in the early evening; drinking coffee and talking. Sometimes I would sit on the stoop and Grampa would tell me stories about growing up in Kentucky, and how, after serving a hitch in the Army, he decided to leave the hills and look for work down in what he called "the flatlands." The back porch had large screens to keep out the bugs and an old sofa that I would sleep on during the Dog Nights of August.

In the basement was a fairly modern furnace that had an auger that transported coal from the bin to the firebox. A trapdoor on the side of the house allowed the delivery man to stick a chute down and fill our coal bin without having to go into the house. There was also a staircase on the side of the house leading from the basement to the outside. Now that I was getting older and able to do more "manly" chores, one of my responsibilities was to haul the cinders and ash from the furnace, up the stairs, to the rear corner of the house. The pails of ash and cinders found a new home in a fifty-five gallon drum from which   the top had been removed. In the dead of winter Mom would put scoops of cinders on the driveway when it got icy. The basement also housed a wringer washing machine sitting next to a set of galvanized rinse tubs. Clothesline ran the length of the basement, situated as far from the furnace as possible.

On the left side of the house was an extra large driveway that we shared with the neighbors on that side. Hedges ran along the right side of the yard, thick and thorny and six feet tall. The front yard was a small rectangle, bisected by a red brick walkway leading from the public sidewalk to the porch. By comparison, the backyard was three times the size of the house. Clothesline was stretched along the right side between two T poles set in concrete. A fence that was half chicken wire and half slat wood separated the yard from the alley that ran the length of the block. A large gate for vehicles and a smaller people sized gate opened out into the alley. In the left corner of the yard, next to the alley, was an old storage shed that was too small for the car and too large for just the lawn mower. It was just the right size for a lonely boy on a rainy afternoon when his presence in the house was inconvenient. It was in that shed that I learned to love the sound of rain on a tin roof. Next to the shed was an aging box elder tree. When the weather cooperated, leaning against that old tree was my favorite place to read.

For years the neighborhood alleys had provided a regular source of income. Most people used burn barrels back then to get rid of their trash and only put wet food garbage on the curb for the city collector to pick up. The burn barrels, usually 55 gallon metal drums with the tops cut out, sat like rear gate sentinels along the alley. I would cruise up and down these dirt thoroughfares a couple times a week, checking peoples' barrels for empty soda bottles. A two-cent deposit was factored into the purchase price of a soda, redeemable when the bottle was returned. Not everyone wanted to be bothered with keeping track of and returning the empties, so the bottles often ended up in the trash. I had a wagon that I would pull as I hunted for bottles. Sometimes generous people would leave six-packs or even wooden cases of empties next to their burn barrels, knowing some kid like me would come along to salvage the two-cent per bottle deposit. But most of the time I would have to fish the individual bottles out of the burn barrels. People didn't always burn every day and I would have to retrieve the bottle before it got burned and cracked. With the exception of scoring the occasional six-pack or the glorious experience of liberating a wooden case of empties, my usual haul averaged five or six bottles. I would take the bottles home and wash them. Sometimes I would wait until I had a full wagon load, but most of the time I would load a cardboard six-pack holder and carry them down to the corner store. With the twelve cents I would buy a comic book and a couple of pieces of Bazooka Joe bubble gum. I would read the comic book while walking home, my jaw working the gum until my face ached. I would put the second piece of gum next to my mom's place when I set the table for supper.

Then one day my economic world collapsed. I put my six-pack holder up on the store counter along with my comic and the gum, and the lady told me, "I'm sorry Bud. The price of comics has gone up to twelve cents." I was crushed. I put the comic back on the revolving rack, bought the gum and took the dime home. I located an old Miracle Whip jar, punched a slot in the lid and made myself a bank. From then on the pennies went for gum and the dimes went into the jar. I didn't know what I was saving the money for, but I knew I wasn't going to buy any more comics, not at the outrageous prices they were now asking.

One spring my mother took her Income Tax refund check, went down to the local Montgomery Ward's retail store and bought a small chest freezer that, in this house, found a home just outside the door on the screened-in back porch. From then on, except for items like milk and bread, Mom bought groceries in bulk from a warehouse store. She would get a package lot that included five-pound tubes of hamburger, boxes of chicken pieces, an occasional roast, and waxed boxes of frozen vegetables. I hated the brussel sprouts, the cauliflower, and the mixed peas and carrots.

One evening, when I was pushing some mushy cooked carrots around my plate with a fork, Mom said, "Eat your carrots. They're good for your eyes."

"Then how come Bunny Rabbit wears glasses?" I snapped. In my defense, let me say that this had been the third time that week that I had to endure peas and carrots. The freezer was getting low and all the good vegetables were long gone.

Placing her fork gently on the table, Mom leaned back in her chair and cocked one eyebrow at me. "What?"

"On 'Captain Kangaroo'," I explained. "Bunny Rabbit is always getting in the carrots and he wears glasses."

"Two things, Buster Brown," Mom said. She held up an index finger. "One, that's just TV, That's not real." She put her middle finger up, making a vee with the index finger. "And, two, if TV is going to cause you to sass me, that idiot box is going to be heading out the door."

I didn't really believe her threat. After all, she would watch TV almost as much as me. But still, I lowered my head, scooped up a forkful of peas and carrots and said softly, "Sorry, Mom."

Down toward the end of the street, just before it turned into a county blacktop that disappeared into the cornfields, was a small wooded area with a creek running through. It was part of the public golf course, a barrier designed to keep wayward hooks from hitting passing cars. I called the grove "Sherwood Forest." It was there that I first encountered Robin Hood.

We'd been living in an apartment then, one where I didn't have a room of my own and slept on the living room sofa. I liked going into the "forest" on hot summer days, to sit in the shade of the trees along the creek and read. One afternoon, accompanied by a jar of sun tea, a couple stalks of wild rhubarb, and a book, I sat with my back against a large sugar maple with large sturdy branches that reached all the way across the creek. I was wanting to finish Howard Pyle's version of the adventures of Robin Hood. I had read a couple of kiddie books about the Merry Men that were OK, but the librarian had told me that Pyle was the standard by which all other accounts were measured. I had watched Richard Greene play Robin Hood on TV and I had been thoroughly fascinated by Errol Flynn and Douglas Fairbanks up on the silver screen. I had even sat groaning as "The Mickey Mouse Club's Spin and Marty" fumbled their way through the saga.

I must have dozed briefly. One minute, I was looking at a page in my book; the next minute I was looking at twigs and shards of bark covering that same page. I leaned forward to gently brush the debris away, being careful not to smear any of the sap that might have gotten on the page. As I was bent over, something hit me on the back of my neck. I jerked my head around, looking left and right, trying to spot the origin of the ambush. A twig landed on the book in my hands. I looked up.

I looked up and fell back against the trunk of the sugar maple, for there, crouched on the massive branch that spanned the creek, was Robin Hood. It wasn't Richard Greene and it wasn't Errol Flynn. It was the real Robin Hood, the one I saw with my mind's eye. If asked to come up with the differences between this Robin Hood and the Errol Flynn version, I would have been hard-pressed to explain just exactly how they were different. But, none the less, in my heart of hearts, I knew the differences existed. This was no actor on a movie set. This was a pointy-bearded tall man with broad shoulders, clad in Lincoln green, sword on one hip, silver hunting horn on the other. On his back was a quiver of arrows, each a clothyard in length, fletched with the finest of goose feathers. In his hand was an English longbow made from the wood of a sturdy yew tree. The man, now straddling the branch of the maple tree in the small park next to the golf course near where the street hit the edge of town and became the county blacktop, was none other than Robin Hood.

"Ah, my young, drowsy friend," Robin was saying to me. "You should probably close your mouth, lest flies buzz in and out."

"How…how…how?" I stammered, my eyes fixed on the form above me.

"How, indeed," replied Robin. "Have you not heard that Robin of the Hood is a friend to those whose fortunes are not what they should be, the ally of the oppressed, bringing aid to those in need?" His voice had a touch of laughter, as if he found life humorous and the experience of living a treat to be enjoyed.

"But…but…whaaa?" Still amazed, I still stammered.

"Are ye not in need? At least in need of a friend? One could always use another friend." Robin's voice grew softer as he spoke, but his words still carried.

Hearing his words, and the heart behind them, I could no longer look Robin in the face. I lowered my eyes and said, almost in a whisper, "I don't have any friends."

My eyes went back up when I heard Robin snort and say, "What? A likeable looking lad such as yourself?" As I watched, Robin dropped down from the branch and knelt at my side, his hands clasped together around his bow. "How could you not have friends?"

"I don't know," I said, looking away from Robin. "I mean, I try, but I never seem to fit in. I read books. Nobody likes kids who read books. I always answer the questions the teacher asks and the other kids all think I'm weird."

"So, do you know more than the other students?" Robin asked, setting his bow down and leaning back on his heels.

"Not all the time," I said, shaking my head.

"But often enough to advance a grade, perhaps?"

"My mom won't let them do that. She says that as bad as it is now, it would be even worse if I was showing up kids older than me. I get picked on enough as it is."

"It sounds as if your life is a sorry lot," Robin said. He picked up one of the twigs and began peeling it clean of bark.

Startled, I turned to face Robin head on. "No," I said firmly. "It's not like that at all. My Mom loves me. My Grampa loves me. I got food and clothes and a roof over my head."

Chuckling, Robin said, "That sounds like a mother's speech."

"Well, it's true anyway," I snapped.

"Ah, feisty. Tis noble to defend your mother. I'm thinking you have the makings of a man in you." With this, Robin stood. "Well, I must be off. But I shall be about, my feisty young friend." He lifted the silver trimmed hunting horn that hung at his side. "Take heed. When you hear the sound of Robin's silver horn, it means help is near." He lifted the horn to his lips, blew a single, clear tone, then leaped across the creek and was gone.

I sat for the longest time, staring at the spot between the trees where Robin Hood had disappeared. Finally, when the sun had moved far enough west to send shafts of light to where I was sitting, I shook myself, picked up my book and empty sun-tea jar and went home.

I didn't tell my mother. I wasn't in the habit of keeping things from her and it wasn't that I wanted to keep things from her, but how could I begin to convince her of something I hardly believed myself.

CHAPTER TWO

I loved to read. Mom used to tease me that I had been born reading; that when she gave birth to me I came out with a book in my hands. Although I've always known that wasn't quite the truth, I have also known that I started reading real early and as a result read better and had a larger vocabulary than most kids my age. I have also always had the ability to remember most of what I read. Some people are hearing oriented, or learn best through hands-on training. I am and always have been a book person. Mom never complained when I brought comic books home, but she would never buy them for me. She told me they were a waste of time and money, but the main reason was, and I didn't understand this for the longest time, she thought comic books were beneath me. She said if I was going to read things, I should read worthwhile things. Every once in a while the Piggley-Wiggley Grocery Store would have a display rack filled with inexpensive classics; books like "Black Beauty", "The Man in the Iron Mask", and "Robinson Crusoe." Quite often the pages would come out after a couple of readings because the binding was cheap glue with plastic coated cardboard covers. But the words of Robert Louis Stevenson and Mark Twain are the same whether they are found in a 59 cent grocery store book or in a hundred dollar leather bound collector's edition. The books I could call my own were few because money was often tight. But that was OK; there was always the city's public library.

The library was housed in a large stone and block building built during the 1930's. It had "Andrew Carnegie" engraved in big letters above the oak double doors with brass fittings that served as the entrance. To get to the double doors, you had to climb a flight of fan-shaped steps that started wide at the sidewalk and narrowed as they reached the top. There were sixteen steps. I knew that because I had been counting them ever since I first started coming to the library, which was long before I was allowed to check books out. When I was real young, Mom would bring me on Saturday afternoons, her day off from work, and help me make my selections, some for my own reading pleasure and some that she would read to me as I drifted off to sleep. But it had been a few years back since she had read to me. She, somehow, didn't seem to find the time anymore. I missed it; not so much the reading itself, after all I could get through most books faster reading them myself. But I missed the sound of her voice and the way she could make the printed page sound like singing. Now it seemed as if all I heard were orders and complaints, neither of which makes for quality music.

The library had long ago outgrown the building, but instead of adding on, the powers that be just kept rearranging and adding shelves. This made for narrow aisles and created nooks and cubby holes that only the small could access. My favorite secret place was behind a rack of newspapers-on-sticks. In an earlier life it had been a padded window seat, set back in a tiny alcove. But these days you couldn't even tell it was there. The back of the tiered newspaper rack was flush with the walls on either side of the alcove, rose high enough to prevent anyone from looking over the top, and came down behind the newspapers, stopping about twelve inches from the floor. I discovered the window seat by accident, chasing a wayward nickel that had fallen out of my pocket and skittered across the hardwood floor.

I would wait until no one was around, then drop down, roll under the lowest newspaper, and sit on the padded seat, reading by the light coming through the window. The window was dusty. The ledge around the seat was dusty. The seat was dusty except where I had wiped it clean with the seat of my pants. The only part that wasn't dusty was the floor. The janitor obviously swung his dust mop far enough under the newspaper rack to keep the floor clean.

One Saturday afternoon I found a new biography of Abraham Lincoln, my favorite president (this was Illinois, after all). I rolled under the newspaper rack and made myself comfortable. I became so caught up in the book that I was absolutely unaware of the passing of the hours. I also took no notice when the librarian announced that it was closing time. I read and read and read, turning the pages quickly in my passion. I read until I realized that the words on the page were getting hard to make out. I looked out the window in horror to see that the sun had gone down and the street lights had come on. I rolled back out into the aisle and ran to the double doors. A large chain was laced through the crash bars of the doors. Securing the chain was a lock the size of my fist.

"What am I going to do?" I moaned aloud, falling to the floor with my back to one of the doors. "Mom is going to kill me."

"There is always more than one hole to a rabbit warren."

I looked up with a start. Robin was sitting on the desk where books were checked out, his bow in his hand and his legs dangling down the front of the desk. By now I had visited with Robin Hood quite a number of times in "Sherwood Forest," but this was the first time I had seen him anywhere else.

"How…how did you get in here?" I asked, looking around at the locked doors and the closed windows.

Waving his bow toward the lock and chain, Robin said, "These things are not a barrier to one such as I. Where I please to go, I go."

"What am I going to do?" I repeated. "I'm not you. I can't sneak in and out of places."

"Is this a fortress with only one sally-port?"

"Huh?"

"The rear, my boy. Check the rear."

Hearing a noise, I shifted my body to look down the main aisle. When I glanced back, Robin was gone.

Seeing by the clock above the door that it was almost nine in the evening, and figuring I didn't have anything to lose, I got up and started walking toward the back of the library. I had only taken a few steps when I heard a deep voice call out, "Fee, fie, foe, fum. Who's out there?"

"Oh, man, am I in trouble," I said softly. Steeling myself, I spoke louder. "I got locked in."

A man came out of one of the back rooms with a waste basket in his hand. It was the janitor. His expression was stern as he looked me up and down. His voice matched his face as he said, "Out kinda late, ain't cha?"

My words came tumbling out in a rush. "I was reading; I didn't hear them say it was closing time; I'm really sorry; I don't know what I'm gonna do; my Mom is gonna kill me…"

"Whoa, whoa, whoa," the janitor said. "Slow down. No point in having conniptions." He cocked his head to one side and a grin replaced the stern frown. "Yer that Bud kid that's here all the time, ain't cha? Do you got a phone so's we can call yer Ma?"

We didn't have a telephone in the house we were living in at the time. The neighbors would let us use their phone, and would sometimes deliver messages in an emergency, but it was late for small town folks and I didn't think the neighbor lady would like being bothered. I shook my head.

"Well, I can let ya out," said the janitor turning to a door behind which was a stairwell. "But I can't do nothing about yer Ma killing ya. That's yer own hook to wiggle off of."

He led me down the stairs to the basement and opened the rear door. Because of the flight of stairs leading up to the entrance, the basement door was actually at street level. As I ran down the alley to the cross street that would take me home, I could hear the janitor shout, "Pay a bit more attention to the clock next time."

The house we lived in at the time was fifteen long blocks from the library, but I ran all the way and was painfully winded by the time I got home. Stopping at the front gate, I leaned with my hands on my knees, trying to catch my breath. Finally, the pain in my side eased and my heart stopped racing. I stood, squared my shoulders and started up the walk to face the music. I was not looking forward to the tune. As I reached the front stoop, I heard, faintly but clearly, the sound of Robin's silver horn. With that encouragement, I opened the door.

Actually it wasn't as bad as I had feared. I hadn't been spanked in ages, and if anything deserved a whack, I guess this stunt did. Mom was upset big-time and I was grounded from TV for a week, but it could have been worse. The only thing I missed on TV was re-runs. When I told her that I had gotten lost in a book, Mom said, "You know, now that's the one excuse I have no problem believing."

The hardest part came as I was finishing a cold supper. Mom stood beside my chair, rubbing the top of my buzzcut. "I don't know what I would do if something happened to you. I love you, Buddy-boy."

I would have preferred she whacked me. I turned in my chair and put my arms around her waist, burying my head in her apron. "I'm sorry, Mom. I try to be good. I really do."

Gently grabbing my ears, Mom turned my face up toward hers and gave me a soft kiss on the forehead. "OK," she said, letting go. "Time to stop getting mushy. Finish your supper and get ready for bed."

She walked over to the stove to pour herself the last cup of coffee in the pot. Over her shoulder she said, "Just don't do it again, OK. You scared more years off me than I can afford to lose."

"OK, Mom," I said. I bent over my plate to finish the last of my cold meatloaf. As Mom walked through the doorway into the living room, I said, "Mom?"

She stopped, cup of coffee in hand and looked at me.

"I love you too, Mom."

CHAPTER THREE

Second only to the library, my favorite place to go was the Crown Movie Theater. It was on Main Street, in the middle of a block smack in the middle of downtown. Built during the post-W.W. II boom, it had a balcony that ran across the back and halfway up both sides and a stage that hadn't been used since TV had put traveling stage shows out of business. There was a large lobby adorned with posters of upcoming films and framed photographs, some even signed, of famous actors and actresses. Just inside the lobby, past the ticket window was the concession stand. It sold popcorn, soda and candy bars of every description. It also carried bags of chocolate covered raisins, jelly beans and hard candy. My favorite candy tasted like root beer and was shaped like little kegs. Whenever I went to the movies, which was quite often, and had a spare dime, which wasn't near as often, I would buy a bag of root beer kegs. They lasted a lot longer than popcorn and had the added bonus of not making me thirsty the way popcorn did.

The only time the theater didn't run a double feature was when the main movie was extra long, like "Ben-Hur" or "The Alamo." Usually there were two movies, previews of coming attractions, at least one cartoon and sometimes two, and a short feature. Some of the shorts were boring documentaries about the "cutting edge of science." But most of the time they were behind the scenes in Hollywood type pieces.

The local beverage wholesaler sponsored a feature every Tuesday afternoon during the summer. With an admission price of six bottle caps, kids would come from all over the county. Some of the kids would be standing in line by noon wanting to get the best seats, fighting for the first row in the balcony. The films weren't current by any means. Usually they were from the Forties or early Fifties. Sometimes a movie from the late Thirties would sneak in. The Tuesday afternoon program also included a couple of cartoons and a comedy short such as The Three Stooges or Our Gang. This where I was first introduced to Captain Peter Blood, Senator Jefferson Smith, and the Ringo Kid who caught the stagecoach to Lordsburg to shoot it out with Luke Plummer. All for six bottle caps.

The corner store had a chest cooler containing soda pop. Fastened to the front of the cooler was a pronged bottle opener. When someone would buy a soda, they could stick the bottle up into the opener with the lip of the cap hooked over the prong, push down on the bottle and the cap would come off. The slightly twisted caps would fall down into a small box mounted on the cooler under the opener.

Not being able to afford to purchase six sodas a week, I would go down to the store on Monday afternoons, as did many of the neighborhood kids, and ask the store owner for the bottle caps needed for the next day's matinee. It bothered me that I wasn't buying the sodas that the caps were coming from and I wondered if I wasn't somehow cheating the company paying for the movie. But when I asked Mom about it, she said that the company sponsored the film for the tax write-off and to generate good-will in the community. I didn't quite understand any of this, especially tax write-offs, but Mom said that I would learn more about taxes than I cared to know soon enough, and that it was OK to get the caps from the store. It also bothered me that some of the kids used their dad's Schlitz Beer caps, but Mom said it was none of my business and to not stick my nose in where it wasn't invited.

Some of the kids complained that the movies weren't new enough, especially the ones in black and white. But I never complained. I liked old black and white movies. Of course I just liked movies period. New movies, old movies, real old silent "flickers", I didn't care: I liked movies. What I didn't like was the noisy crowd at the bottle cap matinees. They would push and shove, yell at each other across the auditorium, throw things at each other, especially down from the balcony, and in general, just about destroy the whole movie going atmosphere.

Going to the movies was the closest thing I had to a religious experience. It had structure, liturgy and the mystical awe that only the truly devout can appreciate. When the theater got dark and the curtain came open I was transported to a far better place. It was a safe place where bad things happened at a distance; life had happy endings and dads came home from the war. It was watching Anthony Quinn as Quasimodo, opposite Gina Lollabridgida as Esmeralda in "The Hunchback of Notre Dame" that I learned the term that fit my movie going experience to a tee. In the womb of the theater, I found sanctuary.

Beside hunting pop bottles for their deposits, as I got older, I raked leaves in the fall and shoveled snow in the winter. The money went into the First National Bank of the Miracle Whip Jar. I would budget my earnings so they would allow me to go to the movies throughout the year without having to ask Mom for the money. Regular features cost a quarter for a kid and sometimes I would take along an extra dime for the root beer candies. Mom never asked me what I did with my money. She said that it was my own money, I had earned it and as long as I wasn't chasing fast women and smoking cigars I could do what I wished. Every once in a while, after a productive week of lawn raking or sidewalk shoveling, I would say, "Let's go to the movies, Mom. My treat." She would laugh and rub my head and say, "Sure thing, my little man. It's a date."

One time I asked her and she didn't laugh. She started crying and ran into her room. I went up to the open doorway and looked in. Mom was curled up on her bed, hugging a pillow to herself.

"What's the matter, Mom?" I said softly, tears coming to my own eyes. "Don't cry."

"Oh, Bud. Come here, honey." She straightened her legs and patted the side of the bed. I walked over and sat sideways on the bed, one knee on the bedspread, my foot hanging over the edge.

"I'm sorry, Bud," she said, reaching out and squeezing my thigh just above the knee. "I don't tell you often enough how much you mean to me. Sometimes your love is the only thing that makes life worth living."

Later that evening Grampa came over and I could hear him and Mom talking in the kitchen. If my dad were alive, this would have been his birthday. I asked if I could go out in the back yard and look for constellations like the ones in the book on astronomy I had just finished reading. Mom looked real tired as she nodded her head.

This particular back yard had a picket fence with a vine covered trellis over the gate. I went to the gate and leaned against one side, my hands wrapped around a couple of the pickets. I puckered my lips and whistled a note, trying to imitate Robin's horn. I had never called him before and didn't know if he would show up. Within seconds Robin was standing next to me, his crossed forearms resting lightly on the top of the gate. I was relieved.

"Your horn needs work," Robin said.

"Robin, please don't tease me. I'm scared."

"I know."

"It's my mom."

"I know."

"I'm not scared of her. I'm scared for her."

Robin stared off into the distance. "People's burdens are their own. You can, sometimes, help them to carry the burden. But you cannot remove the burden. You cannot ease someone else's pain."

"I know I can't do much for her," I sighed. Turning to Robin, I asked, "Can you help her?"

"Have you told her of me?" Robin asked, continuing to stare ahead.

"I...well...I...sort of," I mumbled, biting my lower lip. I didn't know how to tell Robin that I didn't know quite how to tell anybody about him.

"What she does know of me, does she believe?"

"What do you mean?"

Robin turned to face me. "I can only be of help to those who believe I can be of help. I fear I cannot be of help to your mother." Putting his hand on my shoulder, Robin continued, "Look at me, and pay heed to this. You can be a far greater source of help than I."

I looked up at Robin, bewildered. "But, how?"

"I can only tell you that you will recognize the opportunities when they happen. Trust your heart, my young friend. There is more to knowledge than is found in your books. Sometimes the knowing only comes in the midst of the doing. Wisdom is not of the mind. Trust your heart."

Robin braced his hand on the gatepost, leaped sideways over the fence, easily clearing the picket points, and disappeared in the darkness of the alley. I turned and looked at the kitchen window, the light coming from within in what would normally be a warm and inviting glow. I looked up at the stars, down the alley and then back to the window. I dreaded the idea of going back inside. My mother was in pain and, in spite of what Robin had said; I doubted my ability to do anything about it.

"But I'm just a little kid," I whimpered, my hands stretched out toward the stars. "I don't know what to do. I don't know what to say." The words were no sooner out of my mouth when, on the autumn breeze, I heard the sound I had come to love so well, the sound of Robin Hood's silver hunting horn. Remembering Robin's promise that the sound of his horn was evidence that help was near, I headed back into the house. I hugged my grandfather and my mom, and went into the living room to watch TV until bedtime.

As Mom was tucking me in on the sofa, I said, "Mom, if you ever have need of me, I'll be here."

With a sad smile, Mom said, "Did you get that from Robin Hood?"

"Sort of."

"Well, the next time you see him, tell him I said thanks." Then she turned off the light and went to her own room.

Late that night, I awoke to hear her crying. I wasn't in the habit of using bad words; if I had been I would have cursed God, my dead father, and a world that had no concept of fairness.

CHAPTER FOUR

I can't remember a time when we didn't have a television. It wasn't the same as the movies. It didn't have the majesty and the authority of the dark hall and the large screen, but it had the advantage of being free, or so I thought. When I was a lot younger I thought the wooden box was full of tiny people who existed only to bring me pleasure. I got behind the set one time and peeked through the vent holes in the back, trying to see the little people. I was so insistent about the little people that my grandfather, saying, "Don't ever let me catch you doing this," took the back of the set off with a screwdriver. He pointed out the tubes and the wires and explained that it was like radio only with pictures.

"Some real smart guy," Grampa said, "figured out a way to change the pictures and sound into energy that can be thrown from one machine to another."

"Wow," I said, my eyes moving from the bowels of the box to Grampa and back again. "Like magic."

"Well, not quite magic," Grampa chuckled, screwing the back of the set firmly in place. "It's called science, and it pays a whole lot better than magic."

Long before this summer had rolled around, I had helped Davy Crockett fight Indians, crooked politicians, and the Mexican Army. I had returned to those thrilling days of yesteryear with John Reid, who, although ambushed and left for dead, struck terror in the black hearts of bad guys as The Lone Ranger. Bret and Bart Maverick taught me the futility of trying to fill an inside straight. I had ridden long and hard cleaning up the Old West with Cheyenne Bodie, Bronco Lane, and Sugarfoot. I had studied the art of comedic timing, learning from masters like Jackie Gleason and Sid Caesar. I had loved Lucy, been stumped by the $64,000 question, and had been viewed through the Romper Room magic mirror. Mom called television the "one-eyed baby-sitter." She would say, somewhat jokingly, that I got up early to watch the test pattern that was aired before the stations would officially sign on, so that I could focus my eyes to see the screen better.

I would get up on Saturday mornings to watch Roy Rogers, Circus Boy and Rin-Tin-Tin. Sunday evenings were devoted to Lassie and Walt Disney, and every afternoon through the week was set aside for Cap'n Bob's Riverboat. Broadcasting from Davenport, Iowa, over on the Mississippi River, Cap'n Bob would sit in the wheel-house of the Mississippi Queen and tell lame jokes between cartoons featuring such favorites as Felix the Cat and Popeye. For years I believed that Cap'n Bob was a real riverboat captain broadcasting from a real sternwheeler that cruised up and down the Mighty Mississippi. The idea of anybody deliberately using sets in a studio to deceive a bunch of impressionable kids was unthinkable, and when I learned the truth I was horrified, and, by association, Felix the Cat lost some of his luster.

Long before the term "latch-key kid" came into vogue, I was a latch-key kid. Although, technically I wasn't a latch-key kid because we never locked our door, therefore I never had to carry a key. But, none the less, because Mom had to work, after school let out for the day and during the summer I was pretty much on my own. Mom would give me chores to do around the house, with instructions to "not watch that blasted idiot box" until the chores were done. I have to admit that I wasn't always a very obedient child. Anytime I wasn't absorbed in some book, that TV's magnetic, hypnotic power would draw me under a spell stronger than any voodoo incantation. It was as if the will to resist was sucked right out of me just by entering the living room. Heroin addicts and TV junkies are much the same; whatever it takes to get a fix, no price is too high.

I used to listen for Mom's car in the driveway, quick shut the TV off and head into the kitchen to start supper. On the rare days I hadn't been watching TV, Mom would walk in, set her purse down, walk into the kitchen and give my shoulder a squeeze or rub the top of my head. On the days I had been watching TV; she would come in, set her purse down, stomp into the kitchen and give me a cuff on the side of the head. It took the longest time for me to catch on to her "all-knowing" ability. When she came in, she set her purse down on the top of the TV which was just inside the front door. When doing so, her fingertips brushed the top of the cabinet. If the wood was warm, the TV had just been on. Sherlock Holmes had nothing on my mother.

When color television sets started becoming more widely sold, and more and more programs were advertised as being broadcast in color, Mom would talk about how one day she was hoping to get a color set, if, for no other reason, than to watch the Tournament of Roses Parade on New Year's Day.

Mom worked at a factory that made gloves. She ran an industrial sewing machine, putting knit cuffs on yellow "monkey-face" work gloves. She was paid an hourly base rate with the idea that she would turn out a certain number of gloves per hour. Any amount of gloves over that base number meant she made extra money. She said it was "piece work" because she got paid by the number of pieces of work she did in an hour. On a good day when she had a full spool of thread and the needle on her machine didn't break, she could make as much as an extra quarter or even fifty cents an hour.

I had never known my father. All I knew about my dad was that he had been in the Army and had died in the Korean War. There were pictures in a photo album that Mom kept in her bedroom; black and white snapshots of my parents looking young and happy and in love with life and each other. There was also a hand-tinted 8X10 of my dad in his uniform. I had gone into my mom's room one snowy afternoon, I think I was seven, and I found her sitting on the side of her bed, the album open across her knees. She was crying.

"What's the matter, Mom?" I asked. It always disturbed me to see her cry.

Clearing her throat, she said, "Sometimes I just feel lonely, Bud."

With an insight beyond my years, I asked, "Do you think you'll always miss him?"

"Yeah. Probably."

She shut the album and set it on the bed. Opening her arms, she pulled me close and rubbed the top of my head. "You would have liked him, Bud. And he would have liked you. He would have liked you a lot."

She held me for the longest time, not saying anything, just holding me. Then with a sniff and a shake of her head, she said, "Let's be like Peter Pan, and think happy thoughts." Then she let me go.

She put the photo album in a trunk at the foot of her bed and I never saw her looking at it again. I'm sure she must have, but I never caught her at it.

Leaning back against the box elder tree, I told Robin about my father; about how much it grieved my mom that he was dead; about how I had never had the opportunity to know him. I told Robin that I felt an emptiness; a loss, not having a father in my life.

"Is that why you think so highly of this one you call 'The Duke'?" he asked.

"You mean John Wayne?" I was puzzled that he would bring up The Duke in reference to my father.

"Lads learn manly traits from their fathers." he said. "You appear to think of this actor as your substitute father figure. Is it not true that you desire to walk like him, talk like him, react like him in any given situation?"

"What's wrong with that?" I asked a little upset. After all, John Wayne was my hero. I didn't like anyone, even Robin Hood, putting the knock on him.

"Do you believe that everything that happens in these plays is real? When John Wayne shoots someone is that person really dead?"

"No, of course not."

"So, if that part is not true, what makes any of what he does true? He recites lines others have written for him. He does things others have told him to do. That is what acting is all about. You do not know the real man."

"I don't understand what you're trying to say," I said.

Robin squatted next to me with his palm held out open before me. "Hold your heroes loosely, my young impressionable friend. They are not perfect. They are just men, and as such have feet of clay."

"Then what should I do?"

"Eat the meat and spit out the bones. Be prepared to learn from many sources. Not everything you read or view will be truth. Receive that which your heart tells you is good and noble and leave the rest alone."

"What about you?" I asked. "Do you have feet of clay?"

Robin stood and looked down at me, sadness on his face that I had never seen before. "I make no claims to perfection. I am who I am, nothing more." Then he walked away.

That was the beginning of my understanding of the need for tolerance and acceptance between friends. But I still wished I had a dad.

CHAPTER FIVE

Music was a constant sound in our house. Mom had a radio in the kitchen, as well as one in her bedroom. In the living room was a record player with a spindle that would hold six long-play albums. When one album would finish, the tone arm would swing over to the side and the next record would drop down onto the turntable and the tone arm would set the needle down and play that one through. Then Mom would turn the stack over and listen to the flip sides. I could tell her moods by the records she would play. When Mom was happy, she would listen to Glenn Miller and Benny Goodman. When she was sad, she would put on Patsy Cline and Hank Williams. When she was really sad, she would play Kitty Wells. It got to be that whenever I heard "It wasn't God Who Made Honky-Tonk Angels" I knew it was time to go to my room or the basement or anywhere I could find out of harm's way and be as quiet as possible.

Every once in a while, always on a Saturday night, she would play Ruth Brown, Muddy Waters and B.B.

King. Whenever I heard Mom play blues records I knew that she would be going out in tight clothes and lots of make-up and that I would be spending the night at Grampa's house. It didn't take long for me to catch on to what was happening, and as much as I loved my grandfather and as much as I loved spending time with my grandfather, I hated when those Saturday nights rolled around.

I asked her one time why she didn't listen to rock and roll. Mom snorted and said, "That's not rock and roll. There hasn't been any real rock and roll since Elvis went into the Army and Buddy Holly died over there in Iowa. Even Chuck Berry don't make 'em like he used to."

Both of her radios were tuned to the local country station. I didn't mind country-western, and I even liked some of it, but I also liked the songs I heard artists do on TV; people like Ricky Nelson and the groups that would show up on Ed Sullivan's Toast of the Town. The kids at school would talk about the "Silver Dollar Survey" on WLS out of Chicago. But when I asked Mom if I could listen to the "Survey", she said, "When you buy a radio, you can listen to whatever you want. Leave my radio dial alone."

Grampa had an old floor model radio that stood about three and a half feet tall. It was in a wooden cabinet with an arched top and a lighted dial about the size of a pie plate. Grampa had it zeroed in on WSM out of Nashville. Every Saturday evening he could be found listening to "The Grand Old Opry" followed by the show broadcast from the Ernest Tubb Record Shop, although Grampa wasn't too keen on the current country music. His taste ran back to his Kentucky roots with Bill Monroe, Lester Flatt and Earl Scruggs, and the original Carter Family--A.P., Sara and Maybelle. I learned early on not to even bother asking Grampa about changing stations.

Finally, after an extremely profitable snowfall, I went down to the S.S. Kresge store and paid three dollars and twenty-seven cents (including tax) for a turquoise Japanese transistor radio complete with nine-volt battery and earplug for private listening. From then on, a lot of the dimes in the Miracle Whip jar went for batteries. Grampa told me that I could tell if a nine-volt battery had juice left by touching my tongue to the two posts at the same time. He howled when I did it for the first time. I didn't see the humor in it, but he sure got a laugh.

Whenever I was outside, walking to the library or whatnot, I would put the earplug in my ear; run the cord down the inside of my shirt and slide the radio into my pants pocket. I could do this because when Mom bought my school clothes, she would buy them a little large so that I would have room to grow. Hence, my pants had baggy pockets and I would have to cinch my belt real tight to keep them from falling off my hips. Every fall it was the same thing: a pair of sneakers (Keds), a pair of hard shoes (whatever was on sale), two pairs of slacks, one pair of jeans (never Levi's), three shirts, socks, underwear, and a winter jacket and gloves. I had a hand-me-down stocking cap from Grampa. He called it a Navy watch-cap. By the time the next summer rolled around the hard shoes would have been half-soled, the sneakers re-glued, and the jeans would have holes in the knees. With the sensitivity level that kids in groups seem to always possess, I got teased a lot about my limited wardrobe. I knew better than to ask Mom to buy me new clothes all the time, but even knowing that money was "hard-earned and carefully spent" didn't stop me from sitting with the J. C. Penney catalog and making out "wish-lists."

I took that little transistor radio with me just about everywhere I went. I would sit in the backyard and listen to Cubs games on Chicago's WGN. I would tune in WLS 890 every Friday as soon as I got home from school to find out which song was number one on the "Silver Dollar Survey." Most of the time I listened to WLS. Clark Weber and Dick Biondi and the other disc jockeys were my pals and I believed that anything they said was solid-rock reliable.

One time I took the radio to school, put it on the shelf under my desk top, and ran the earplug cord up the front of my shirt and into my ear. I sat so the teacher couldn't see the earplug. It was autumn and the baseball season was winding down. I probably would have gotten away with it if I hadn't become excited during a Cubs rally in the bottom of the ninth. The teacher came over, saw the cord, and with a look forecasting an early end to my existence, she held out her hand. To the amusement of the rest of the class, I took the radio from my desk, wrapped the earplug around it and handed my most prized possession over to a woman I now viewed as the Wicked Witch of the West. Actually it could have been a lot worse. She kept the radio for two weeks and I had to stay inside and clean chalk erasers and blackboards during recess. Mom had to come in on her lunch break from work to take possession of the radio. She kept it for another two weeks. Four weeks without the "Silver Dollar Survey" and the end of the season for my beloved Cubs was almost more than I could handle. I even missed the World Series, not that it mattered all that much; the Cubs missed the World Series too. I never took my radio to school again.

One day I was sitting by the creek in "Sherwood Forest", listening to a ballgame, when Robin came and sat next to me. Waving his hand toward the radio in my lap, Robin said, "Tis a marvel. News, weather, entertainment, just about everything one could need to know about what's happening in the world."

Pleased at Robin's observation, I said, "I love it. I really love it. I think I'm gonna be a disc jockey some day."

"Yes," Robin continued. "It is truly a marvel. You never have to go out and be with people when you have one of these."

Now I was confused. Turning to Robin, who was staring at the trees on the other side of the creek, I said, "What do you mean?"

"One must be a friend to have a friend. You take as your friends those things that you believe will never let you down. Movies, television, this radio, even the books you read and treasure so dearly. You risk nothing embracing them as your friends. After all, if you find a book distasteful, you never have to read it again."

"But, you're my friend. I said.

"True, I am your friend." Robin turned his head to look at me, a slight squint in his eyes. "But are you my friend?"

I was floored. "What do you mean?" I asked

"What would you risk for me?"

"What do you want me to do?"

"No," Robin said, wagging his finger. "Tis not that simple. To be a man means sometimes doing what people want and need without them ever having expressed their want or need."

Now I was really confused. "But how am I supposed to know what people want if they don't tell me?"

"When you start to care more for people than you do for things, then you will start noticing what people don't or can't tell you."

Breaking Robin's eye-contact, I looked down at the radio. "I don't know if I really want to like people," I said softly.

"Ah. Why is that?"

A thousand memories rushed through my mind. "People do mean things. People say mean things. They say mean things to me. They say mean things…" My voice began to break. "…mean things about my mom." I pulled my knees up to my chest, wrapped my arms around my legs, lowered my head and began to weep.

After some time passed, Robin said, "Do you ever talk to your mother about this?"

I looked up, wiping my cheeks with the backs of my hands. "No," I sighed.

"Why?"

"I don't want to make her feel bad. Some of the things they say are dirty."

"Are they true, these things you have heard?"

Something inside of me broke. Pounding my fists on the ground, I screamed, "I don't know. Don't you get it? What if they are true? What am I gonna do?"

"Who said you must do anything?"

"She's my mother." Now I was angry and I made no attempt to hide it. How could he be so dense?

Calmly Robin said, "She is thy mother. She is not the Blessed Virgin. She is not one of the Saints living in stained glass. She is a grown woman. She is a human. Humans err. If it be the case that she is in error, which has yet to be proven, you must know two things. One is that you cannot fix her. But even more important is that whatever she might or might not be doing that would be unseemly, it does not change the truth that she loves you. And love you, she most certainly does."

Standing, Robin looked down and said, "Do not sit in judgment upon your mother. I would wager she has had plenty of that in her days."

After Robin left, I reached down to where the radio had fallen from my lap and turned it off. It wasn't until much later, when I heard the sound of golfers swatting brush at the far end of the grove looking for a lost ball that I got up and went home. I didn't sleep well that night; Robin's words ricocheting inside my brain. "She loves you. Don't judge. She loves you."

The following Saturday, I came home from the library and heard B.B. King's "Sweet Little Angel" coming through the front door. I stood on the porch and looked through the screen. Mom was in a slip, dancing across the living room from the kitchen to the bathroom. She was sipping from a tall glass that I knew from experience contained Bubble-Up and cherry vodka. Her hair looked nice, like she had just gotten back from spending a buck and a half at the beauty operators'. She jerked her head around when she heard the screen door open and close.

"Oh, Bud," she said. "You're home. How would you like to go to Dad's tonight?"

"Sure, Mom," I said. She must have heard something in my voice. She turned fully around and looked at me.

"Are you OK?" she asked.

All of a sudden I knew I could truthfully say, "Yeah, Mom. I'm fine."

I headed for my bedroom. As I reached the door, I turned to see her still standing in the hall watching me. I gave her a smile, a genuine from the heart smile, and said, "You know, sometimes I think I must be about the luckiest kid in town, having you for a mom. I love you."

She reached in and set her drink on the top of the toilet tank. Then, swaying to the music, she came up to me, tilted my head up with her palms on my cheeks, and said, "Bud, you are a slippery-tongued rascal. What do you say; we both go over to Dad's and listen to the Grand Old Opry with him? Maybe we can interest him in a game of 500 rummy."

CHAPTER SIX

There was a bakery in town that made cream horns; flaky pastry cones filled with French cream. I liked the light, white French cream better than the heavy, yellow Bavarian cream. It was not unusual for me to wake up on Sunday morning and find that Mom had gone out early and bought a Sunday paper and a dozen cream horns. She would make a pot of coffee, pour it into a vacuum bottle and bring it and a cup, the paper, and the pastries back to bed with her. When she would hear me stirring about, she would call, "Get yourself a cup, Bud, and come in here." Those occasions were some of my most favorite times. I wasn't allowed to drink coffee except on those Sunday mornings. But the coffee, exciting and "grown-up" as it was, wasn't what made those mornings special. It was during those times that I got an understanding of what made the world go around, at least from my mother's vantage point.

Mom would bunch her pillows up at the head of her bed, and as we ate cream horns and drank black coffee, she would read the paper. I would look at the color funnies and check the movie schedule and the TV listings, marking my viewing choices with a colored pencil. When Mom would come to an article of particular interest, she would read it aloud, and then we would discuss the subject of the article. Mom's questions to me nearly always started with "Why do you think...?" The topics would range from the space race to the pennant race, with an emphasis on politics. She approached local, national and world events with equal enthusiasm. "What happens in South Africa," Mom would tell me, "could very well have just as much impact on your life as what happens on the south side of town." She would also read the editorial page to me, including the letters to the editor. Mom said that I needed to hear different sides of issues, and accept that issues had more than one side, so that when I was older I could be an intelligent citizen and not "some knee-jerk bone-head with a closed mind."

One Saturday afternoon I was standing at the library card catalog jotting down the Dewey Decimal number for a Bruce Catton book on the Civil War, when I felt someone brush up behind me. I looked over my shoulder at a wrinkled sport shirt. I lifted my eyes to a smiling face behind a pair of wire-rim glasses.

"Quite a weighty volume for someone your size isn't it?" the smiling man said.

Shrugging my shoulders, I said, "I read one of his other books. I really liked it."

"Good show," said the man, as he opened another card catalog drawer. "I have a particular fondness for Catton myself."

Later, as I was sitting at a table hunched over the book, the man came and sat across from me. Putting my finger on the page to hold my place, I looked over at the man.

"Like it?" the man asked.

"Yeah," I said, grinning.

"Going to check it out?"

"I can't. It's an adult book and I only have a kid's card."

Arching an eyebrow behind his glasses, the man asked, "How old are you?"

"Eleven. Well, almost eleven."

"And you're reading adult books?"

"Well, I kinda outgrew kid's books, and there isn't much in-between. Sometimes my mom will come and I can check books out on her card."

He leaned back in his chair and cocked his head to one side. "Do you understand what you read?"

"Most of it. I used to have to sit here with a dictionary, 'cause I would find a lot of words I didn't know. Now I just try to figure them out as I go. Mom says that's using the context."

"Sounds like your mother knows what she talking about. That's how I learned to understand words. Words are my business."

Sticking his hand across the table, he said, "I'm Dan O'Brian."

It rang a bell. I told him my name as I shook his hand, and then said, "Dan O'Brian, the guy in the paper?"

Sitting back with an amused look on his face, O'Brian said, "Do you read my stuff?"

Leaning forward with my arms crossed on the open book, I answered, "Some of it. We don't always get the paper. But my mom gets the Sunday paper a lot, and she always reads your column. She didn't like you blasting the school board the way you did a couple weeks back. But most of the time she likes you."

Laughing heartily, O'Brian said, "Oh, well. Can't please everybody."

An elderly librarian walked over to the table and leaned down close between us. "I should have known it was you, Daniel O'Brian. Don't be corrupting this young man now. Although he's as much like you were at his age as anybody could be. I swear he reads more books than you did, only more quietly. So hush, both of you."

She was smiling as she straightened up. "It doesn't surprise me to see you two together. No, it doesn't surprise me at all."

She was chuckling to herself as she walked away. We both watched her settle down at her desk.

"I wish I was like you," I said.

"Were, not was," corrected O'Brian.

We both turned in our chairs to look at each other.

"Why do you want to be like me?" The smile was gone from O'Brian's face.

"You're popular. People know you. People pay you money to write. What could be better?"

"Do you write?"

"Sort of," I said, thinking of the many wastebaskets I had filled with the crumpled remains of my writing efforts. "It's not very good. Most of what I write is pretty boring."

"What kind of life do you have?"

"What do you mean?" I asked, puzzled.

"The best writing, the writing that connects with other people is an extension of who you are down deep inside. It rings true to the reader when it's true to you. Even the most outrageous science fiction has at its core an honesty, a reality that's fueled by the author's life experiences. Do you understand that?"

"I think so. All good writing is at least a little bit autobiographical."

"Exactly. So, what do you do? Do you play sports? Make music? What? What is the passion in your life?"

I shook my head with every question.

"Don't tell me," he said. "Let me guess. You have the TV Guide memorized. You go to the movies every chance you get. And you read a lot of books."

All of a sudden I was ashamed of my life and didn't quite know why. I hung my head and stared at the book in front of me.

"Hey," O'Brian continued, his tone softer. "I'm not telling you this to make you feel bad. I was just like you, except it was radio instead of TV when I was a kid. And believe me; you don't want to be like me."

Startled, I looked up. "Why not? You're the top writer on our paper."

O'Brian sighed and this time he was the one who looked away. After a few seconds he said, "I'm thirty-two years old, and I've gone as far in my profession as I can."

Looking back at me, he went on, "You know what I am? I'm a spectator to the game of life. I write about what other people do without ever having done any of it myself. You can't just sit on the sidelines, kid, and watch life go by. I don't have a life, not by any real definition. All I have is a job. I'm not knocking the job I have, but there are guys cranking out books and working on major-market newspapers who can't write their way out of a paper bag, and I'm still here."

He took off his glasses and pinched the bridge of his nose. His eyes stayed shut as he continued. "I write for the paper I grew up reading. Every time I try going somewhere else, I always end up coming back. The hometown fish that couldn't make it in the big pond. Believe me, it's not how well you write; it's having something to write about that's a part of you, your life, your experiences. A giving away of something of yourself to your reader. Do you know what my column is? It's me expressing other people's opinions."

Opening his eyes and leaning across the table, O'Brian's eyes were wide. I didn't quite know whether it was from passion or because he didn't have his glasses on. Maybe both. His voice was gentle as he said, "I'm not putting you down. I'm really not. It's just that

I've been there and in many respects I'm still there. But life is not a spectator sport. You have to be a player, not someone who is sitting on the sidelines watching it happen. It isn't enough to root for the home team. You have to be the home team. Don't be afraid to grab life by the ears, hop in the saddle and ride it for all its worth. When you can do that, then you'll have something to write about. When your teacher has you give her an essay on how you spent your summer vacation, it isn't going to be enough to say you sat under a cherry tree and read books."

Once again I was slumped in my chair staring down at the pages in front of me.

"I don't really do anything." My voice was barely above a whisper.

"What do your friends do?"

"I really don't have any friends."

"Why does that not surprise me? I didn't either when I was your age." O'Brian massaged his forehead with his fingertips. "For Pete's sake, I don't really have any friends now. There's people I hang out with, but I wouldn't go so far as to call them friends. They don't know me, not the real me. And I don't know them. I've spent my whole life putting up a wall and now I don't know how to climb over it."

My face felt hot and my throat was tight. I was afraid to say anything as I watched O'Brian adjust the glasses on his face. It was as if my whole life had been laid out before me and there was nothing about it worth looking at. O'Brian stood up and walked around to my side of the table. Putting his hand on my shoulder, he said, "Some final advice, Bud. Learn what it means to be a friend, and friends will find you. That's a lesson I wish I had learned a long time ago. Maybe it's not too late for me, maybe it is. I don't know. But I do know it's not too late for you." He gave my shoulder a farewell squeeze.

As I watched Dan O'Brian, Ace Reporter, walk away, I wondered how a man so gifted could be so defeated so early in life. He was only a couple of years older than my mom and I couldn't picture her throwing in the towel anytime soon, if ever. Out of the corner of my eye I saw Robin leaning against a book stack, his elbows propped up on the shelf behind him. He lifted his palms and shrugged his shoulders. I don't know whether to interpret the gesture as "I don't know what to say" or "What do you do now?"

No longer captivated by Bruce Catton's prize-winning prose, I closed the book, got up from the table, motioned with my head to the door and Robin and I began a slow, silent walk home.

CHAPTER SEVEN

No matter where we lived when I was a little kid, I was always in the part of the district that sent their kids to Jefferson Elementary School. That means I had the same group of classmates from kindergarten on up.

I think I got off on the wrong foot with the rest of the kids when, as a five-year-old, I recognized Beethoven's "Moonlight Sonata" when Mrs. Harper, our kindergarten teacher, played it for us on the piano. Mom didn't listen to a lot of classical music, but she said she liked Beethoven's "passion and energy." "Moonlight" was one of her favorite pieces and she played her recording of it every Sunday afternoon for years.

It also didn't help that I was way beyond the "Dick and Jane" books in my reading and comprehension level, could write simple sentences, and could do basic addition and subtraction. In elementary school, there are good reasons and bad reasons to stand out; academic achievement in not a good reason, at least from the kids' perspective. One day during recess I was called something I had never heard before. At supper that night, I asked Mom, "What does 'brown-nose' mean?"

She dropped her spoon into her stew and looked at me with eyes like an owl, big and round and bugging out. "What?" she said loudly. "Where did you hear that?"

"One of the kids at school said I was a 'brown-nose'."

Mom dropped her chin to her chest and slowly shook her head. After a bit, she looked up at me with real sad eyes. "I'm sorry to have to tell you this Bud, but some kids are going to be mean. They're going to do mean things. They're going to say mean things. Not because you're done anything to deserve it."

Mom never did explain what "brown-nose" meant. I had to find out from an older, wiser, more worldly fourth-grader.

What Mom did do was go in and talk to Mrs. Harper. Pretty soon terms like "Momma's boy" and "teacher's pet" started making the rounds of the playground. Kids started avoiding me because they "didn't want 'the Rat Fink' to get them."

It wasn't long before my recess routine became one of finding an out of the way place to curl up with my peanut butter sandwich and a book.

On the last day of my kindergarten year Mrs. Harper planned a party, complete with a clown and ice cream. I missed out because my tonsils chose that particular time to flare up and I was stuck in the hospital to have them removed. When I woke up after the surgery, Mom was sitting there next to my bed reading a magazine. My throat hurt and she gave me an orange Popsicle. She told me that my throat would hurt for a few days and that even after I got home from the hospital I would have to eat soft foods for awhile.

On the day she brought me home, Mom asked me what I wanted for breakfast the next day. I said, "Wheaties." Usually Mom bought store brand cereal, but every once in a while she would buy Wheaties as a special treat. I figured if any time in my life deserved a special treat it was having my throat slit, so I asked for Wheaties. It didn't occur to me that Wheaties wasn't really classified as "soft food." But Mom put some Wheaties in a bowl, covered them with milk and stuck the bowl in the refrigerator. The following morning they were one big soggy mess, but I sat in front of the television watching Captain Gallant and eating Wheaties for breakfast and I was happy.

Every day at noon the city fathers would sound a civil defense siren. This alarm was a test to insure that should the Commies attack; the people would have enough time to get to their fall-out shelters or other designated areas of safety. We would frequently have drills during class time. The principal would stand in the hallway with a bullhorn and say, "This is an air-raid test." And the students would file out into the hall, away from any windows so as not to be injured by any possible flying glass, sit with our backs against the solid concrete block walls, put our faces down between our knees and cross our arms over the tops of our heads. A couple of times during the school year we would be shown civil defense movies in our classrooms. The teacher would set up a 16mm projector, pull the blinds and we would learn all about what to do should we be on the street and see a mushroom cloud on the horizon. "Stop, Drop and Cover" were the watchwords of the day. I don't know about any of the rest of the kids, but for days after one of these training films, I would pay extra special attention to every airplane I heard passing overhead. The Reds weren't gonna take this All-American boy by surprise.

Current events were covered by a four page newspaper called The Weekly Reader. The teacher would usually hand them out on Friday afternoons. Once, we were herded into the gymnasium/lunchroom where a large television had been set up on the stage. Like the rest of the country, we were privileged to witness Alan Shepherd blasting off from Cape Canaveral. Little did we kids know that our world would never be the same.

Another thing that happened a couple of times a year was the arrival of the Scholastic Book Club fliers. The Scholastic Book Club sold inexpensive paperback copies of books printed with the youthful reader in mind. Whenever the brochure showed up, I would take it home, check to see how many dimes I had in the Miracle Whip jar, decide how many of those dimes I could part with, and then make my selections. Books by certain authors always got my attention. I liked Glenn Balch's horse stories and the car books by Henry Gregor Felson. I did, however, learn to shy away from anything that had the word "abridged" in the description. I spent a whole quarter on a copy of Alexander Dumas' "The Three Musketeers" only to find that at least a third of the book had been chopped out. I guess they figured the edited part was over most kids' heads, and they were doing kids a favor, but I felt cheated.

Grade school teachers seem to make a lot of fuss about holidays. We would wear Halloween costumes and eat candy in October, make turkeys by tracing the outline of our hands just before Thanksgiving, and construct heart covered mail boxes for Valentine's Day. However, Christmas had all the rest of the holidays beat. We would sing songs about Rudolph, Saint Nick on the housetop, and every once in a while a song about Baby Jesus. On a Friday evening in late December the parents would come and sit through a couple of hours of what might loosely be called music. Each class would make a presentation and then everyone would eat cookies and drink cider provided by the PTA, while the school janitor dressed up as Santa Claus would hand out candy canes to all the kids.

When I was in the second grade I was invited to a luncheon put on by a local businessmen's service organization. Mrs. Harris made it sound like I was being rewarded for something. She was pretty vague about why, but she had me believing I was pretty special. A big car came, picked me up and took me to the local hotel. The hotel had a meeting room that had been converted into a banquet hall. I was given a name tag for the front of my shirt and a man in a nice suit introduced himself and said he was my "host" for the day. We sat at a long dining table with a bunch of other kids and their "hosts." After roast beef and mashed potatoes with a large glass of milk to wash it down, the lights were dimmed and we watched a Little Rascals movie. Next came ice cream and chocolate cake. When dessert was over, each of the kids was called by name and the kid went over to a large Christmas tree where a guy in a Santa suit handed the kid a wrapped present. The tag on my gift said that it was from my "host." I thanked him the way Mom had taught me and opened my present. It was a model airplane kit; a P-40 like the Flying Tigers used in China during World War Two.

When I got back to school, Mrs. Harris had me stand in the front of the class and show them what I had been given. During the afternoon recess I was showing the kit to a couple of kids on the playground, when a little girl said, "You just got that because you're poor."

"What?" I said, bewildered.

"My mom told me all about it. My dad was there being a 'host' to some poor kid like you. They ask the teachers to tell them who won't have a nice Christmas because they're poor, and they take the kid out for a nice meal and give them something so they won't have to go without. It's called charity. You're a charity case."

I asked Mom about it that night during supper.

"Am I a charity case?"

"What?"

"Was I given a special party and a Christmas present because we're poor?"

"Oh, Bud," Mom said, setting her fork down on her plate. "Is that what you were told?"

"Some of the kids were talking at recess."

"Kids do talk, don't they?"

"Is it true? Am I a charity case?"

Mom got up and went over to the stove where she poured herself a cup of coffee. Sitting back down at the table, she said, "It is true that we don't have a lot of money. When I was asked about you going to this dinner and getting a gift, it never crossed my mind that it would turn out like this. Somebody wanted to be nice to my son and I said 'Yes'. I never meant for it to hurt you. I'm sorry."

Later that night I put my coat on and walked out back to the burn barrel and pitched the model airplane kit in with the rest of the trash. The magic of Christmas was tarnished. It used to be about the Baby Jesus and the gifts of the Wise Men. Now it was about the getting of stuff and the spending of money. The Great and Magnificent Oz was revealed to be nothing more than a silly little man working levers behind a curtain. Some of the magic did finally return when I had children of my own, but I never allowed them to go to fancy dinners with strangers who gave them gifts. My revulsion to getting something handed me by strangers was so deeply ingrained that even applying for college scholarships was something I could never bring myself to do.

CHAPTER EIGHT

I awoke late one evening, hearing voices coming from the kitchen. I slipped out of bed, eased my closet door open and sat with my ear to the wall just opposite the kitchen table. I now had no problem making out what my mother and grandfather were saying.

"Really, Dad." Mom sounded frustrated. "We're doing fine."

"But, Lil, come on." I had never heard anger in my grandfather's voice before. It scared me to hear it now. "He's not a little boy anymore. One of these days he's going to catch on...I mean the catting around...the boyfriends. All of it. I've tried to not interfere with how you live your life..."

"And don't start now," Mom said harshly.

"One of these days he's going to hear the truth about his father."

"Dad, stop right there."

"It's a small town, Lillian. People talk."

They were speaking over the top of each other now, their voices getting louder.

I looked up to see Robin, arms folded across his chest, a frown wrinkling his face.

"Are we spying now?"

Getting up out of the closet, I made a keep-it-down gesture. "Sshhh."

Shaking his head, Robin said, "This is not right. Tis not a noble act."

"They're talking about me," I said, trying to keep my voice low.

"That changes nothing. Tis a knave's deed, to breech someone's privacy. I expect better of you."

I scrambled up to the side of my bed as I heard the doorknob rattle. Robin was gone by the time Mom came through the door.

"What are you doing up?" she asked, glancing at the open closet door.

"I was just gonna go to the bathroom," I lied.

"Then go," Mom said, a gruffness to her voice that made me uneasy. "Then get back to bed and get to sleep." She stepped over to the closet and shut the door.

Coming out of the bathroom, I could hear Grampa and Mom.

"There's a real problem here, Lil," Grampa was saying. "He talks to himself."

"A lot of kids have imaginary friends."

"Four-year-olds have make-believe playmates. Wake up, Lil. He's gonna be eleven here real soon. It isn't right. You have the makings of a serious problem on your hands. I think you need to get a professional opinion. How do you know there isn't something hereditary?"

"OK, Dad. That's enough. Just drop it. I am not sending my son to a shrink."

I heard her chair legs squeak and figured I had best not get caught listening, so I slid as quietly as I could across the hall floor and into my room. As I lay in bed I could still hear their voices. Even though I couldn't quite catch the words, I could make out the tone. It pained me beyond belief that the two people I most loved would be arguing about me. I turned to face the wall, pulled my pillow against my face, and wept.

CHAPTER NINE

We never ate out during the winter. Sometimes Mom would get take-out chicken and French fries from the diner near where she worked. But most of the time Mom would leave some meat out to thaw and leave instructions for me about peeling potatoes and whatnot.

Summer was a different story. We would get into Mom's Studebaker on Friday as soon as she got home from work and changed her clothes, drive over to the A&W stand by the highway, and order tenderloin sandwiches and frost covered mugs of root beer. Mom would roll the driver's side window up just enough for the car hop to hang the food tray on the side of the car. Quite often, after supper, we would go to the drive-in theater. Mom would have a bag of snacks that she had just picked up at the store waiting in the backseat. Popcorn was the only thing we ever bought at the drive-in's concession stand because no matter how we tried, we could never get our popcorn to taste as good as the theater did.

Mom was always the most relaxed when she was behind the wheel of the Studebaker. She loved driving. Sometimes we would get in the car and she would just drive, no particular destination, just up one county blacktop and down another. It was as if controlling that massive car gave her a sense of power that she never had in any other part of her life. Mom would turn the car radio on and sing along with Patsy Cline, Lefty Frizzell and Webb Pierce. When a Johnny Cash tune came on she would make her voice go real low, so low it would croak. I always laughed when she did that. Mom would smile, reach her hand over to rub the top of my head and say, "One of these days your voice is going to drag bottom like that, Buster. Just you wait and see."

But there was always a point when she would turn the radio off and we would talk. When she was behind the wheel, relaxed and feeling in control, I could ask Mom just about anything and she would not get upset.

This particular Friday evening, as we were finishing up our root beer, Mom said, "There's a new John Wayne movie at the drive-in. Do you want to go? Or is that a stupid question?"

I had figured that's where we would end up when I got in the car and saw the bag of snacks in the backseat. But I didn't tell her that, I just said, "Sure, Mom. Sounds like fun. Let's go."

She honked for the car hop to come and remove the tray with the empty mugs and the wicker baskets that had held the sandwiches. Then she put the car in gear, backed out of the parking spot and turned onto the highway.

"We got some time to kill before dusk, how about we take a spin around the town?"

She turned on the radio, heard the beginning of the news broadcast and clicked the radio back off again. As she drove, I sat with my hands between my knees, staring at my inter-laced fingers. Mom glanced over at me and said, "Something on your mind, Bud?"

Sighing a heavy sigh, I turned in the seat to face her. (This was way before seatbelts.) I could see Robin in the backseat directly behind my mother, out of her line of sight. His face was a blank mask under his feathered cap. He nodded at me as if to say, "Yes, now is the time."

I'd never had to drum up as much courage as it took to say, "Mom, tell me about my dad."

Her eyes shot over to me and then back to the road. "So," she said sternly. "You were listening the other night, weren't you?"

How I wished I could go back sixty seconds and keep my mouth shut, but like Grampa used to say, "You can't unscramble eggs." I hung my head and said, "Yes. I know it was wrong and I'm sorry." Then I looked back up at her, my eyes moist. "But I want to know about my dad. I need to know about my dad. What is it that Grampa's afraid somebody else might tell me that you won't?"

Half under her breath, Mom said something that sounded like, "Well, Lil. It has most certainly hit the fan."

Raising her voice so that I could hear her more clearly, she said, "I guess it's about time, Bud. You have a right to know, but, God, you don't know how I hated for this day to come."

Pulling into a turnout on the side of the road, she took the car out of gear and set the brake. Mom turned in the seat to face me, a sadness in her eyes that made her look as old as time itself. Then, as if she couldn't talk to me while looking at me, she turned forward to stare out the front window. In the backseat, Robin put his finger to his lips and made a pushing down motion with his other hand. I took my cue and waited silently, knowing somehow that the story would come easier for her if I didn't force it.

When she finally spoke, her voice was a flat, unemotional monotone. "Your father was the sweetest, kindest man I've ever known. We met in high school. He was two years older than me. We dated all through his junior and senior year. Then he went off to the state university. That mess over in Korea had just started up, but they weren't drafting college kids, so we didn't pay it much mind. I had just gotten out of high school, and when he would come home on the week-ends we would go out. He was old enough to drink and I hadn't been carded for years. We were in some beer joint down by the county line, dancing and carrying on, and we both had too much to drink. Some jughead said something dirty about me and your dad beat the guy pretty bad.

"The judge gave him a choice, go to jail or join the Army. A month later he was in boot camp. He came home on leave and then shipped out to Korea. He was already overseas by the time I realized you were on the way."

Her knuckles were white gripping the steering wheel. Her eyes were closed and her chin had slumped down onto her chest. Looking in the backseat, I saw Robin nodding and gesturing for me to now say something.

Taking a deep breath, I said, "Did he die in Korea?"

"No, he didn't," she sighed, her eyes still closed. "Part of him did, down deep, the part that made him…him. When he came back he was changed. So changed. You were a little over a year old and he wouldn't hold you. He wouldn't hold me. He wouldn't…he wouldn't do a lot of things. He said his hands were dirty. 'I can't touch you,' he would say, 'my hands are so dirty.' And he would cry. I would find him curled up in a ball and he would be sobbing."

By now the tears were forcing their way through her clenched eyelids, smearing her makeup and leaving mascara streaks on her cheeks.

Her voice took on a moaning tone as she continued. "He ended up in an Army hospital. They were evaluating him, they said. The next thing you know, there was an Army Major standing in our living room, telling me how sorry he was, telling me they didn't know how it happened and how he was going to have somebody's ass in a brown paper bag. But it was all just words, words that didn't help a damn bit."

Opening her eyes, Mom turned to look at me. "Your father was in a lot of pain, in his mind and in his heart. And he couldn't take the pain anymore. Somehow he got a hold of a razor blade and slit his wrists."

I thought of what my grandfather had said. "Was my dad crazy?"

Mom reached over and pulled me to her bosom. "Oh, honey. He was sick. He was sick in his mind, but it wasn't something he passed on to you. He was fine until he crossed the Pacific and went to that damned peninsula."

We were both crying now, and as if to prove there is a God in heaven who weeps over the heartaches of man, rain started spattering the windshield.

It was quite a while before Mom pulled a hanky from her purse and wiped her eyes. She put the car in gear, turned on the wipers and lights and headed home. John Wayne could wait for another day. We drove in a silence broken only by an occasional subdued whimper and the echo of the memories of shattered hearts.

As Mom pulled into the driveway, I stirred in my seat. She turned off the lights and the wipers and killed the engine. The interior of the car was dark, the only light around coming from a distant streetlamp. I could barely make out Mom's face when she turned toward me. "Was there anything else?" Her voice was husky.

There was something else; something that I had wondered about for years and had never had the nerve to ask. This night seemed to be the right time even if it wasn't going to be a good time.

"How come we don't get any money?"

Mom jerked upright, her eyes wide, catching the far away street light. "What do you mean?"

"I was reading a magazine article a while back about a thing called 'survivor's benefits'. How come we don't get any, Dad being in the Army and stuff?"

Mom looked at the ring on her finger and then started crying all over again. "Oh, Bud," she said. "I am so ashamed. I don't know how to tell you this. I loved your father, and he loved me. He gave me this ring when he was home on leave, but, well, the truth is we never did get married. Not officially. Not legally. And because there was no record of him being your father, not to mention him not being my legal husband, the government figured they didn't owe us anything. There was a small insurance policy made out to me, but it wasn't much."

Mom reached out and gripped the steering wheel and through clenched teeth said, "In the eyes of a lot of folks, that makes me an evil woman."

She turned to me again. "I'm sorry, Bud. My sins have come, and will continue to come and roost on your doorstep."

"You've never said much about Dad's mom and dad, other than they're not around anymore."

"When it rains it pours, huh? You sure you want it all?"

No, I wasn't sure it was what I wanted. What I wanted was for everything to be hunky-dory, but I knew that wasn't going to happen. What I told her was, "I really need to know, Mom."

Reaching out to take my hand, she said, "I know, honey. I know."

Sitting up straight in the seat, she pulled me close and draped her arm across my shoulders.

"They were your basic, run-of-the-mill farm folks. They worked hard, went to bed early and didn't hold with any kind of carrying on. They blamed me for what happened to your father. I can hear his mother now, 'If he hadn't taken up with that honky-tonking chippie, he never would have ended up in Korea, 'cause he never would have got in trouble in the first place.' I can kind of see their reasoning, kind of. Particularly his mom, now that I have a son of my own. They'd had another son who died of diphtheria or something when he was real young. All the love she would have divided between two sons, she gave your dad. If things hadn't gone bad over there, I think she would have come around. Your dad would have brought her around. She would have learned to love you at least, and maybe learned to accept me."

"They didn't love me?" I murmured, hurt by events that I never knew had ever happened. That these things had taken place years ago made no difference, the hurt was new for me.

Squeezing my shoulder, Mom said, "You have to realize, Bud. There was a lot of pain going around. People say and do a lot of hurtful, stupid things they later regret when they're in pain. I said a lot of mean things to them, too. It's a two-way street, stupidity."

Snuggling up under her shoulder and taking her hand, I said, "They're dead, aren't they?"

Tightening her arm across my chest, Mom was silent for a spell. Her body shook slightly as she wrestled with the memories and emotions. Finally she exhaled forcefully through her nostrils.

"They went pretty quick. She passed away within a couple of months of your dad. No will to live, I guess. Actually, your grandfather, your other grandfather, your dad's dad, he came around once in a while after that. He was sort of awkward and shy at first, kind of like he was afraid he was betraying his wife or her memory or something. But he would hold you and tell me stories about your dad as a boy. I have a picture somewhere of him holding you on his lap, him smiling and you just a laughing something fierce. But he died. Black lung from working the coal mines when he was younger. He didn't have any other relatives. He left everything to you, with me as executor of his will. I was given the liberty to spend the money however I thought best. That's how I got this car. There was an estate sale and I took what money was left over after the lawyers got done, added some of that government insurance money, and bought this old bucket of bolts, new off the lot." She patted the steering wheel as if to say she was only kidding with that "bucket of bolts" comment.

"So there's only you and me and Grampa?" I asked.

"Well, there are some shirt-tail cousins down in Kentucky that I haven't seen in years. But, for the most part, yeah, it's you and me and Dad." Loosening her grip, she said, "Hey, you know, I think there's an Alan Ladd movie on the late show. How about you grab the grub and we get in out of this nasty, old weather?"

Mom grabbed her purse off the floorboard and holding it over her head like a miniature umbrella; she scooted around the front of the car and onto the porch. I was right behind her, carrying the bag with the chips and cookies and stuff. Just before I went in the door, I looked over and saw Robin standing at the corner of the house, under the eave, out of the rain. It was as if he were keeping watch, silent and strong and vigilant.

Mom and I watched the local news and then the movie. At least, I think Mom may have been watching the movie. My eyes were pointed in the direction of the TV screen, but my mind was in another place and another time, wondering what could make a man feel so defiled that life itself no longer had value. With the illogical logic many kids use, I wondered if my dad's "dirty hands" wasn't somehow my fault. I was on the verge of asking Mom, but when I looked over, I saw her asleep in her chair. The dredging up of yesterday's horrors had fatigued her more than any amount of physical labor could have done. I touched her shoulder, giving it a gentle shake. When she was almost awake but not quite, I had her stand up. I led her to her room, pulled back her bedspread, helped her out of her shoes, and for the very first time ever, I was the one tucking someone else into bed for the night.

We weren't what one would call a church going family. I wasn't sure what I believed about God, other than the idea that there probably was one, but I knelt down next to my mother's bed and in a whisper said, "God, Mom can use some peace, if it's OK with you. And my dad, well, you probably know more about that than me. But, wherever he is, tell him I'm sorry I never got to meet him. Thank you."

I closed my mother's door as quietly as I could, turned off the TV and the living room lights, and walked back out on to the front porch. I sat in Mom's old rocker and listened to the rain come down. God still crying. Well, there's an awful lot to cry about, I thought to myself. Robin squatted down next to the rocking chair.

"It's not your fault, you know."

I was continually amazed at his ability to read my mind.

"How can you be so sure?" I asked.

"You were a year old. How could you be at fault?"

"I don't know. Maybe he was disappointed at what he found."

"And maybe he was disappointed at what you might have found as you got older."

I pulled my heels up onto the rocker seat and wrapped my arms around my legs.

Robin rested his fingertips on the arm of the rocking chair. "Your mother's testimony was that he had changed. Maybe he loved you too much to allow you to see him as he had become."

"Shouldn't that have been my choice, whether I wanted to be with him or not?"

"Perhaps. But you can't change what was, or what is. You can only move toward what might be. If you must think back, think back upon him as the man who loved your mother. And leave it at that."

Robin stood as I got up from the rocker. I didn't know how to thank him for helping me put things into perspective. I wanted to tell him how much it meant, him always being here for me, but the words just wouldn't come. So I said a simple "Good night" and went in and went to bed.

Surprisingly enough, I had no difficulty falling asleep. And with that, my day ended.

CHAPTER TEN

I was mowing our back yard. We had one of those rotary push mowers. It wasn't as easy as a gas powered machine, but the noise of the gas engine would have drowned out the Cubs game on the radio; I considered it a fair trade.

"Thy grandfather is dying."

I looked over to see Robin with his legs crossed at the ankles, leaning with his left shoulder pressed against the side of the box elder tree. Robin's right hand rested on the silver hunting horn.

I walked over, squatting down and turning off my radio, I picked up a twig and began peeling the bark from it.

"Did you hear what I said?" Robin asked.

"I really don't want to talk about it, Robin."

"But you must, my young friend," Robin said softly. "'Tis a festering sore upon thy heart."

Tears were forming in the corners of my eyes when I finally looked up at him. After a few moments of trying to collect my thoughts, all I could manage to say was, "But, why?"

Why, indeed. Why did he have to die? Why does anyone have to die? Why now? Why? Why? Why? My mind wanted to explode from the unfairness of death, the pieces being hurled to the far reaches of the universe, each piece screaming "Why?"

"'Tis part of the cycle of life. One is born, by God's grace lives a productive and honorable life, and then goes to one's eternal reward. Such was the design from the beginning. Such is the way of all living creatures."

The phrase "but what about me?" kept repeating in my brain. Tears were flowing freely now, as I stood to my feet. Part of me recoiled at the anger that came boiling out. I threw down the twig and the fist full of bark. My temples were throbbing and my jaw was shaking. I felt like Lon Chaney, Jr. turning into the Wolfman. I just wanted to howl; howl at the moon, howl at the world, and most of all, howl at death, challenging its right to claim my grandfather.

"It isn't fair," I snarled.

Robin straightened with both hands on his hips.

"Fair?" he said. "What is 'fair'? 'Fair' is the festival that occurs every autumn over at the City Park. Is it fair that you've had your grandfather all to yourself while millions have never had him or any like him for a moment in their lives? Why is it you cannot enjoy the blessings you have while you have them? Why must you focus of that which you do not have?"

I wanted to shake him. If I had been older or taller or stronger I probably would have tried. "I don't know what I'll do when he's gone." I was continuing to snap and snarl. "What will Mom do? She needs him!"

"She does not need him, lad," Robin said calmly. "She has not needed him since she reached her maturity. She might desire to have him present, but do not confuse desire with need."

Was he talking about Mom, or, was he talking about me? When do wants turn into needs and where is the line between the two? Is it wrong to have wants? Was it wrong to want to have my grandfather alive and well and a part of my life? Why does life have to be so hard and so full of questions I couldn't answer? I felt deflated.

I pulled the crew neck of my t-shirt up to blot my eyes. "I feel like such a baby," I sighed.

"Why is that?"

"Men don't cry."

"Did you read that in a book?" Robin said with a snort. He put his hand on my shoulder and said. "Tears, or the absence of tears, these are not what define manhood. A goodly man, a noble man, a true man is one who loves as well, as greatly, and as fervently as he wages war. Love that is never acted upon is not love, and a heart that cannot express grief is a stony, shallow heart—a heart unbefitting a true man."

Robin stood erect, cocking his head to one side and staring off into the distance. "I must go. My help is required elsewhere. Be at peace, dear one. Be brave and be at peace."

Putting the silver horn to his lips, Robin blew a single clear note, and then he was gone.

CHAPTER ELEVEN

I was sitting on the front porch steps looking at the newly arrived fall and winter catalog when Mom got home from work. She was humming cheerily as she came up the walk. "Hey, Bud." Her voice almost had a song in it. "Whatcha got there?"

"J.C. Penney," I said.

"Got your wish-list going?" she teased, stopping with one foot raised on the first step.

Looking up at her, I said, "Mom, what's the matter with Grampa?"

The smile went out of her eyes and her shoulders drooped a bit. The hint of song was gone when she said, "Let's go in. I need to get off my feet."

I tossed the catalog into the magazine holder next to Mom's easy chair and followed her into the kitchen. She put a pot of coffee on the stove to perk, and, to my ever-loving surprise, set two cups on the table. I slid into my chair and put my fingers through the cup handle. I glanced up when I heard her clear her throat in a nervous sort of way.

"You're more of a man than you know," she said. She turned toward the backdoor and looked out the screen. "You've had to fend for yourself an awful lot, and done a better job than most grown-ups. And I know I don't have any right to say this, but now I'm going to need you to be more of a man than you've ever been."

She avoided my eyes as she went over to the stove. She folded her arms across her chest and leaned one hip against the counter, staring at the flame under the coffee pot. When the coffee began that hiccupping sound and started bubbling up the spout, she shook herself and blew like a winded foot-racer. She turned off the burner, picked up the percolator with an oven mitt, and carried it over to the table. I watched her pour coffee into both cups and set the pot down on a hot pad. I waited until she got settled in her chair before I spoke.

"Is Grampa sick? Is he gonna die?"

Mom picked up her cup with both hands and blew across the top of it before taking a sip. She set the cup down and stared into it as if expecting to see a message written by the oil swirling across the top of the hot liquid.

"As you have noticed," she said wearily. "Dad is not doing well. Not doing well, that's an understatement." Looking straight at me, she said, "Yes, Bud. Your grandfather is dying. We've known it for awhile. Dad didn't want to tell you. He didn't want you to worry."

Surprisingly, her eyes were very dry, almost too dry. I wondered if it was because she had wept so much in private that the tear reservoirs were empty. I reached across the table and brushed her knuckles where they jutted out from clenching her coffee cup.

"What is it?" I asked.

Mom let go of her cup and squeezed my fingertips. "He has a cancer that can't be operated on. I don't know. Crying out loud, I thought doctors could do anything these days! I mean, they got a cure for polio and they can't do anything about this. It's a crappy world, Bud, a crappy world." Mom spread her other hand over her face and pinched her temples with her thumb and pinky finger.

"When is he going to die?"

"A year ago they told us six months. Who knows? Soon, I suppose, from the looks of him."

"What are we going to do?"

"Move on. Get by." She dropped her chin to her chest and said softly, almost as if to herself, "God, I don't know. I really don't know."

She lifted her head, let go of my hand and leaned back in her chair. "I was just a little older than you when Mom died. Dad has always been here for me. No matter what happened, Dad has been a rock. The Rock of Gibraltar. Steady. Solid."

She hunched her shoulders like she was trying to work a crick out of her neck. "It has not been easy, being my father. How I wish I could change so many things."

She refilled our coffee cups.

"He loves you, Bud."

"And I love him, Mom. I don't want him to die."

She pinched the bridge of her nose. "I wish it were that easy, amigo."

Sighing, she said, "This is where I need you to be strong. He's in a lot of pain in his body. But that would be nothing compared to the pain in his heart if he knew that you know that he's dying. You can't let on."

Later that week Mom came home early from work and told me that my grandfather had been hospitalized. I washed up and put on a clean shirt and my only pair of pants that didn't have holes in the knees. It was a silent drive to the hospital. As she was pulling the Studebaker into the visitor's parking lot, Mom said, "Remember, Bud, you can't let him know that you know."

I was determined in my heart of hearts to give my grandfather comfort however I could. That determination showed in my voice as I said, "Yes, Ma'am," unintentionally sounding a lot like John Wayne.

Together we walked through the entrance and up to the reception desk. Mom asked for Grampa's room number. The receptionist looked at me and said, "I'm sorry. The boy will have to wait down here in the lobby. No one under fourteen is allowed upstairs. It's hospital policy."

Mom had learned long before not to dicker with underlings. She told me that the lower a person is on the totem pole; the less flexible they are about whatever power they possess. Mom asked if she could talk to whoever was in charge. The receptionist spoke quietly into a telephone and after a few minutes an older woman got off the elevator and approached the desk. She was dressed entirely in white; shoes, hose, dress, apron, and little cap with wings that flared out behind her ears. Her name plate, pinned to the top of her apron identified her as the "Head Nurse."

"May I help you?" she said in tones as starched as her little cap.

Taking her by the elbow, Mom said, "May I talk to you privately?" They moved off to the side, their heads close together. When they returned, the head nurse took a clipboard from a rack next to the reception desk, jotted a few lines, and said to the receptionist, "I believe the situation calls for a little leniency today. Go ahead and give the young man a visitor's pass."

Wide-eyed at this breach of procedure, but compliant in the face of higher authority, the receptionist had us write our names on a second clipboard. She handed up playing card sized pieces of paper with VISITOR printed in large block letters. We fastened the passes to our shirt fronts with straight pins. "Be sure to return here and sign out when you leave," the receptionist told us. She said we should take the elevator to the third floor and stop at the nursing station just across from the elevator to ask for directions to Grampa's room.

We got the directions and walked down the hall. I hadn't been back to the hospital since I had my tonsils out when I was five but I remembered the smell. The place smelled funny; almost like the building itself was sick and was taking some kind of awful medicine. We slowed as we neared Grampa's room. I reached out and took Mom's hand and she looked at me. We squeezed each other's hand, gave each other a firm nod, and stepped up to the door. There was a curtain that didn't quite reach the floor drawn around Grampa's bed. Beneath the hem of the curtain we could see a pair of white nurses' shoes moving about. Mom patted lightly on the open door. The nurse stuck her head out from behind the curtain. "We'll just be a moment. We are not quite presentable."

Grampa's voice sounded raspy when he said, "What do you mean we, woman?" This was followed by a gasp and some heavy wheezing. His breath had a whistling sound to it.

"Don't strain your chest," we could hear the nurse saying. "You better behave now, you old rascal, or I'll have to send them away."

Grampa said something that sort of sounded like "you evil witch." But I wasn't sure. However, the nurse was chuckling as she pulled the curtain aside. "He's all yours," she told us.

We stepped through the doorway and to the side to allow the nurse to pass. The nurse leaned into Mom as she reached the doorway. "Don't let him talk too much. And if you need me, just pull that white cord on the wall. It turns on a light at the nursing station."

"Thanks," Mom said with a slight smile. "I appreciate everything you're doing for him."

The nurse reached out and patted Mom on the forearm, giving her a wink and a nod.

"Hey, Bud," Grampa whispered from the bed. "How's my favorite grandson?"

The hours making faces in the mirror paid off as I worked up a smile and stepped over to the bed. "Actually, I think I'm your only grandson."

"A mere technicality that's not my fault."

With feigned shock, Mom moved over to the bed and playfully slapped at Grampa's hand. "Dad," she said with starchy tones not unlike those of the head nurse. "We are not amused."

There was an awkward pause as father and daughter looked at each other. Then, with a smile, Mom shook her head and said, "You are an old rascal, an old hillbilly rascal. Somebody should have horsewhipped you a long time ago."

"Yeah, well, they missed their chance."

This exchange gave me an opportunity to study my grandfather. It had only been a couple of weeks since I had last seen him, but the changes were drastic. It was almost as if he didn't have any meat, any muscle, any firmness at all. His skin was dry and hanging loosely on his face. The bones in his hands were so visible it was like looking at an x-ray. But his hair was combed. He was freshly shaved and his breath smelled of peppermint. When he looked at me his eyes were clear and his gaze steady.

"How you doing, partner?" Grampa was whispering and taking very shallow breaths, his chest barely moving. "Getting ready for school?"

"School's not for another three weeks, Grampa," I said, smiling. "There's plenty of time."

"Time for what?"

Time for what? I asked myself. Time to say good-bye maybe. Time to watch you waste away to nothing. Time to watch you die. I couldn't say any of this to my grandfather. My head came up as I heard the sound of Robin's silver horn through the open window.

Grampa was tapping my hand. "Hello, Bud. Are you still here?"

With a quick shake of my head, I said, "Yeah. Um...Well, there was something I was wanting to ask you."

"Sure, Buddy boy. Ask away."

"You know that old bike in your shed?"

"Yeah. The one you didn't want to learn to ride."

"Well, I think it's about time I learned. I was wondering if you could teach me when you got out of here. That way I can ride over to your house after school and we can play cards until Mom gets off work. Or maybe even I could get a paper route or something. What do you think?"

My grandfather's eyes misted up as he said, "I would love that, Bud. You and me, just like Heckle and Jeckel."

"Mutt and Jeff."

"Abbott and Costello." We both smiled at our well-loved, well-used routine.

The nurse was standing in the doorway. "I'm sorry," she said, "but, it's time."

Mom turned to me and said, "Why don't you say good-bye to your Grampa, and wait for me at the nurse place."

I leaned my face close to Grampa's and rubbed our cheeks together. "I love you, Grampa. We'll do that bike thing when you get out."

Reaching up to cup the back of my neck, my grandfather pulled me close. "Yeah, Bud. You and me, as soon as I get back on my feet."

Mom pulled us apart and pushed me toward the door. "Go with the nurse now, honey, and I'll be right out."

With a wave, I stepped through the door and turned down the hall, the nurse beside me. When we reached the nursing station, the nurse looked down at me.

"I could get in trouble for asking you this, but how much do you know about your grandfather's condition?" she asked.

I looked down the hall toward Grampa's room, my heart telling me that I would probably never see him again. In a monotone I said, "Enough to know he's never going to teach me to ride a bicycle. He's never going to show me another card trick. He's never going to offer me another NeHi or another stick of Blackjack gum." I looked up at the nurse. "I know more than he thinks I know. I know enough."

With a sad smile the nurse put her hand on my shoulder and gave it a light rub. "You're a brave young man."

Reaching up and taking her hand in mine, I said, "I had a good teacher, even if he was a rascal at times."

Then I started crying.

Early the next morning, just before sunrise, my grandfather passed away.

Mom used my school clothes money to buy me a new white shirt, an already tied long black tie that slid under the collar wings and clipped over the top button of my shirt, new black pants and a pair of shiny black shoes. Two days after he passed away, I sat in the front row at the funeral parlor and listened to a minister that I had never seen before say nice things about Grampa. I wondered how this minister had gotten to know my grandfather so well. After the service at the funeral parlor, Mom and I got in the back seat of a fancy black car and followed the long car carrying Grampa's casket out to the cemetery. I had a difficult time thinking of that casket as holding my grandfather. My grandfather had been so strong and full of life. The body in that casket bore only a passing resemblance to the man I had known and loved.

Another service was held at the side of the open grave. I knew my grandfather had served with Black Jack Pershing during the War to End All Wars, but still, I was surprised to see a representative of the local Veterans of Foreign Wars chapter stand in front of the casket and give a brief presentation about the decorations Grampa had earned. My grandfather had never talked about it with me, but it sounded like he had been quite the hero. At the end of the presentation three men in uniform stepped forward. They put carbines to their shoulders and fired into the air. An American flag was folded into a triangle and presented to my mother. As the casket was being lowered into the open grave, I heard a horn in the distance. "Robin?" I thought, looking around. I noticed other people looking in the direction of the horn as if they heard it too. Instead of a clear single note, the horn played "Taps." I gathered it was part of the military honors being shown my grandfather by a thankful government.

I stood as people came walking by in a line, hugging Mom and shaking my hand. Mom told people to stop by Grampa's old house, that there would be coffee and sandwiches and stuff. After everyone else left, Mom and I got back into the rear seat of the fancy car. The driver would take us back to the funeral parlor so we could get the Studebaker and drive it to the reception at Grampa's house. As we were pulling away from the gravesite, I looked back through the rear window. Robin was standing where the VFW guy had stood, at the head of my grandfather's grave. Robin's head was bowed and his hands were folded in prayer.

CHAPTER TWELVE

The following Monday afternoon I was sitting on the front porch steps cleaning the dirt out from under my toenails with a twig. At my side was a jar of sun-tea and my trusty radio. The WGN announcer was describing the action taking place in the friendly confines of Wrigley Field where my beloved Cubs were battling our arch-rivals, the St. Louis Cardinals. I was trying to imagine what it would be like sitting in the bleachers behind the bricks and ivy, catching an Ernie Banks home run. The idea of doing it without Grampa took some of the bloom from the rose, but even so it seemed a quest worth pondering.

My daydream was rudely interrupted by the "aawwaak, aawwaak, aawwaak" of a large truck's back-up warning horn. It sounded like it was coming from the other side of the tall hedge. I scurried to the corner of the yard next to the sidewalk and saw a Global Van Lines moving truck backing up into the driveway of the house next door. The house had been sitting vacant for months but now it looked as if that would no longer be the case. A Rambler Cross Country station wagon was just pulling up to the curb in front of the house.

As I watched, a tall, barrel-chested man with freckles and short red hair got out from behind the wheel. The man put his hands flat on his lower back and stretched backwards like he was working out the kinks of a long drive. Then he straightened up, put his hands on the roof of the car and looked at the house. Leaning down to stick his head through the open car door, he said, "Well, gang. Let's go take a look at our new quarters."

The other car doors opened. From the front passenger side came a tall, curvy woman with hair the color of maple syrup, all shiny and brown with gold highlights. Two little brown-haired girls who looked like they were probably twins got out of the backseat and stood on the sidewalk next to the woman. The man walked around to the rear of the station wagon and cranked down the back window. A boy who looked like he could be about my age, with short red hair and Buddy Holly glasses climbed over the tailgate. He murmured something to the man, who said, "That's not a bad idea, sport."

The man looked over toward the moving van, then at the front of the house and finally over to where I was sticking my head around the hedge. "Hey," he called. "Would you do me a favor, young man?"

I shrugged my shoulders and stepped out on to the sidewalk.

"Do you live there?" the man asked, pointing to my house.

"Uhh, yeah."

"Well then, we're going to be neighbors. Come on over and let us introduce ourselves." The man waved a beefy hand toward the group on the sidewalk.

I walked over to the group and the man stepped up from the street to join us. He put his hand out and said, "I'm Big Jack Anderson."

My hand was swallowed up in the slab of meat hanging from the end of his arm. I told him my name, thinking, "Man, this guy's got arms like Popeye." There was even an anchor tattooed on Big Jack's freckled forearm.

"This is my wife, Mona," Big Jack said, putting his arm around the tall woman's waist. "These are the twins, Debbie and Dotty. They're six. And this is my shipmate." He put his other arm across the boy's shoulders and hugged him to his side. "I used to call him 'Little Jack', but I don't think I can do that much longer. So I guess it's just plain Jack. He just turned eleven."

Just plain Jack and I nodded at each other.

The woman, Mona, squeezed Big Jack's hand then pulled away. "Is your Mama home, sweetie?" She had a slow Southern accent, like honey being poured over biscuits. It reminded me of Scarlett O'Hara's voice but without the hard edge. I could have listened to it for hours.

"No, Ma'am," I said. "She's at work. She'll be getting home about four-thirty or quarter to five."

"Oh, really?" I half-expected her to say "fiddle-dee-dee."

"Mona, you can do your socializing later," Big Jack said. "Right now we have got a ton of unpacking to do."

"Dad," Jack said. "What about the picture?"

"Oh, yeah." Turning to me, Big Jack said, "Would you take our picture? One of us standing in front of our new house? I'll set it up and everything. All you have to do is aim the camera and push the button."

They stood on the front step leading up to the porch and I took their picture with a well-worn old Brownie box camera, holding it at waist level and looking down at the viewfinder screen built into the top.

When Mom got home from work she commented on the car in the next door driveway. I told her about the moving van which had long since left, and described the family, ending with, "That big guy sure can talk a lot." Together we went next door to welcome the new family to the neighborhood.

That evening, and every evening that week, Mom went to the house where Grampa had lived. She was sorting through his belongings, setting things aside to keep and marking the rest for an estate auction to be held the following Sunday afternoon.

A couple of days after the Anderson's moved in I heard music coming from next door, but it didn't sound like it was coming from a record player or a radio. I looked around the edge of the bushes and saw Jack sitting on a stool on their front porch with a small guitar across his knee. Jack saw me and said, "Hey," in a friendly tone.

"Hey," I said back.

"Come on over," Jack said with a wave.

I went up to the first step and leaned against the hand-rail post. I nodded toward the guitar. I had never seen one up close before. "Is that yours?" I asked.

Hugging the guitar tight, Jack said, "Yeah. My dad got it for me for my birthday. That was a month ago."

"It looks kinda small."

"It's a three-quarter size. I was learning on Dad's guitar, but it's way too big for me right now. When I get older I'll get a full-size, maybe even an electric."

Images of Chuck Berry and Buddy Holly and a ton of other guitar players flashed across my mind. In awe, I said, "I never knew anybody that played guitar before."

"Dad is teaching me," Jack said. "He learned in the Navy."

"Your dad was in the Navy?"

"Yeah," Jack said. "He retired a little while back. He said he wanted to put roots down as far from the ocean as he could get. So we ended up here."

I sat down on the top step. "Where were you living?"

"San Diego, in Southern California. Before that it was Virginia. I even lived in Hawaii for a little while, but I don't remember it much. We moved around a lot. I was born in Florida. Pensacola, Florida. Were you born here?"

"Yeah. I haven't been any place. Not Chicago. Not St. Louis. Not any place."

"What's your dad do?"

I looked down at my feet and rubbed my knees with my hands. In a quiet voice I said, "My dad's dead."

Jack set the guitar down gently on the porch flooring and came and sat across from me on the top step. "My mom's gone, too; not dead gone, just gone. Mona's not my real mom, and the brats aren't really my sisters. Mona and Dad got married last year."

We both looked at each other. After a bit we both turned and looked out toward the street, our thoughts too private and personal to share. At least I know mine were. "Got any comics?" Jack finally asked.

"My mom doesn't buy me comics," I told him. I didn't tell him I was still boycotting the price increase.

"I got some new Marvels that I picked up while we were traveling," Jack said. "Would you like to see them?"

"What are Marvels?"

"Marvel Comics. The Fantastic Four. Spider-Man. Don't you know about Marvel Comics? Where have you been?"

"Stuck out in the middle of nowhere." The same place I'll end up, I thought to myself.

Jack stood to his feet. "Wait here," he said. Picking up his guitar, he went into the house. A few minutes later he came out with a cardboard box. He set the box on the porch and plopped down cross-legged next to it. "Man, I got 'em all," he said, opening the top of the box. "DC. Harvey. Archie. I even have some Classics

Illustrated." He was pulling comics from the box as he spoke.

"Check this out." Jack said, a comic book in his outstretched hand.

It was a copy of Disney's "Davy Crockett, King of the Wild Frontier."

"Wow." I said, almost with a reverence, as I reached out and took the book in my hand.

"That's been out of print for a long time," Jack said. "But look at the cover. That's what makes it so special."

Scrawled across the picture of Davy Crockett with Betsy, his rifle, in his upraised hand, was the name, "Fess Parker."

All I could do was sit there, my mouth wide open, staring at the autograph.

"Dad took me to Disneyland right after Mom left. Fess Parker and Buddy Ebsen were there. But I couldn't get Buddy's autograph. Man, there was a crowd you wouldn't believe."

He took the comic book back and held it lovingly in his hands, a smile splitting his freckled face. Placing it off to the side, Jack said, "Dad says I should wrap it in wax paper or something so it doesn't get ruined.

"Except for that one," Jack told me, "you can borrow any of my comics that you want to."

"Mom would have a fit if she came home and found me reading comics," I said.

"Then read 'em here." Jack said, as if that solved everything.

A little while later, Mona Anderson came to the front door carrying a tray with two glasses of milk and a plate of Hydrox cookies. "Can you get the door, Jack?" she asked. When I heard those sweet magnolia tones, I briefly wondered if I could get her to leave Big Jack and run off with me. She was almost better than Maureen O'Hara as an object of idolatry. After all, Maureen O'Hara never brought me cookies and milk.

Jack hopped up and opened the door. He took the tray and set it down next to the box of comics. "Thanks, Mona. I mean, Mom. I mean…" his voice trailed off.

"Don't worry about it, honey," she said through the screen door. "You just call me what you're comfortable calling me and it will all work itself out." We could hear her footsteps as she walked away from the door.

"Man," moaned Jack. "Dad wants me to call her 'Mom', but I forget."

"How long has she been your mom?"

Jack made himself comfortable in that way that kids have that looks so uncomfortable to grown-ups. "Since last summer," Jack answered. He dunked a cookie in his milk and popped it into his mouth. Between bites of cookie and sips of milk, he told me his story. "My real mom left when I was five. My gramma stayed with us, watching me when Dad had sea duty. He would be gone for months, cooking on a destroyer. Then he met Mona a couple of years ago. I don't rightly know what happened to her husband, but it sounds like he was some kind of low-life. Anyway, they got married and Gramma decided she wanted to move to Phoenix and live in something called a retirement community, some place just for old folks."

Feeling a need to make a personal contribution of my own, I said, "My Grampa just died. Last week."

"Oh, man."

Clearing my throat, I said, "Yeah, well. That's life."

"What did you say your dad did?" I asked, changing the subject.

"He cooks."

"Cooks?"

"Yeah," Jack said. "And he's really good. He cooked in the Navy for twenty years, starting when he was seventeen. Gramma signed papers to let him get in right after Pearl Harbor. He decided to get out when he hooked up with Mona. 'Get out while the getting's good,' he said. Something about some place called Viet Nang or Viet Nam, Viet Something or another. He said he didn't want to go through another hassle. Anyway, he gets a retirement check every month. He was looking in some restaurant magazine and found an ad for some place here that was for sale. He came and looked at it and used his savings to make a down payment." Laughing, Jack said, "I figure I'm gonna be bustin' suds 'til I'm out of high school."

"What?"

"Bustin' suds. You know, doing dishes."

We both chuckled and went back to eating cookies and reading comic books.

Later, after supper, as I was "bustin' suds", I told Mom what all Jack had said.

"Well, hon," Mom said. "He sounds like a nice kid. But don't be spending so much time over there that you become a bother, OK?"

"Sure, Mom," I told her.

The following Saturday was my birthday. I was now eleven. I would not be having a party, what with Grampa gone, but the truth is, who would I have invited anyway? Mom made pancakes topped with strawberries and whipped cream for breakfast. As she was finishing her coffee, Mom said, "I want you to come over to Dad's place with me this morning. I need to finish getting ready for the sale tomorrow and there's some things of his that I know he would want you to have."

The drive over to Grampa's house seemed like the longest I had ever taken. Even the ride to the cemetery hadn't been as painful. The numbness I had during the time right after Grampa had passed away had gone and the loss became more real with every familiar street sign. By the time Mom turned the corner and headed down Grampa's old block, I felt like I was in a giant bear hug. I wanted to run the other way as fast as my ratty old Keds could take me.

Mom pulled into the driveway and got out of the car. She walked up to the front stoop, pulling a key ring out of her purse. She turned and gave me that one lifted eyebrow look. I slunk down in the seat until my eyes were level with the bottom of the car window. Why is she making me do this? I wondered. I was trying to make it as obvious as possible that I really didn't want to be going in there, but she just stood there waiting. Having played the waiting game often enough with my mother, and knowing that she held all the good cards, I finally opened the car door and trudged up to the stoop. I walked through the door and stood looking around the small living room. It was like something from a dream. The room was familiar in a hazy sort of way, but I felt like it was a totally new place that I had never been in before. The house was incomplete without Grampa. The world was incomplete without Grampa.

There were boxes stacked everywhere, with contents lists taped to them.

"Take the ones next to the door," Mom said, "and put them in the trunk."

I lifted the top one, marked "Photo Albums" and walked back out to the car. Three trips later and the massive trunk was only half filled. "OK, Mom," I said after the last trip. She called from the bedroom in the back of the house. I found her sitting on the edge of Grampa's old bed, an open suitcase beside her.

"I know most of his clothes are pretty old-fashioned," she said, placing a pair of new looking Levi's in the suitcase. "But jeans are jeans anytime, and one day these'll fit. The same with boots." She held up a pair of glossy black cowboy boots with hand-tooled eagles on the shafts. The thought of filling my grandfather's boots had implications that I was not prepared to accept, but I nodded my head anyway. Anything to get done and get out of there.

Mom pushed the suitcase to the side and patted the bed next to her. "Come over and sit with me," she said.

Once I got situated, she reached over and took a cigar box from the night stand. She leaned close and put it in my hands. "Open it," she told me. My hands were as frozen as my heart and my mind debated whether or not I should obey. My heart was winning until I saw Robin standing in the bedroom doorway motioning for me to go ahead and open the box. I took a deep breath, exhaled loudly through my nostrils and lifted the lid. My eyes grew wide as I saw the items inside.

A fog rolled in; it must have because my skin felt clammy and all I could hear was the sound of the ocean in my ears. "Dad always wanted you to have this," Mom was saying from a distance. She lifted a heavy pocket watch from the box. It was silver with a push button in the center of the winding stem. Pushing the button caused the front cover plate to swing out on a hinge. On the inside, opposite the watch face was a picture of me and Grampa taken the previous Christmas. I was wearing a black and red, Roy Rogers style cowboy shirt, the kind with smiley pockets and fake pearl snaps instead of buttons.

The fog moved on as I closed the watch back up and set it on the bed. Reaching into the box, I lifted out a stag-handled jack-knife. My grandfather had carried it for as long as I could remember. It had two blades, the larger of which locked into place when opened. I looked at Mom.

She shrugged her shoulders. "I never liked the idea of you carrying a knife when you were a boy," she said. "But I guess you aren't a boy any longer. Anyway, Dad was of the opinion that you needed a good knife, that all men need a good knife. Just don't plan on taking it to school."

The next item in the box was a leather pouch with a zipper along one side. The pouch clinked when I picked it up. I set the cigar box off to the side and undid the zipper. The pouch was full of coins; silver dollars, Indian head pennies, buffalo nickels and a large gold piece with twenty dollars stamped on it. "That is a genuine double-eagle. It's worth a whole lot more than twenty dollars," Mom said. "Dad wasn't really a coin collector, but he knew that some coins might become collector's items down the road. You hang on to those and by the time you're an adult, you might have a nice little wind-fall there." I vowed then and there that I would have to be pretty hard-up before I would part with any of my grandfather's coins. My desire was to be able to pass them on to my grandson.

I looked over at the nightstand and saw a leather case similar to a wallet but longer and folded over lengthwise. Mom followed my eyes and picked up the leather case, untied the thong wrapped around it, and flattened it out. It was an old-time document carrier.

"Dad didn't much believe in banks," Mom said. "I found this in the back of his refrigerator. He figured if there was ever to be a house fire; the fridge would still be standing. So he kept his important papers in this case with some oil cloth wrapped around it to keep out the moisture." She sighed and I saw her lick her lips. "When I found this you could have knocked me over with a feather." Her voice broke and she caught her lower lip between her teeth. "Oh, Dad," she finally said.

My mother took a legal looking paper from the pouch and unfolded it. "You have to understand something, Bud. Dad offered me money a lot over the years. In my pride and stubborn arrogance I kept turning him down. What I am now beginning to understand, looking at you, is that a parent feels their job is never done as long as there is something, anything, they can give their child. I'm just now realizing that Dad's efforts were not designed to control me, but to bless me.

"Dad found the house we've been living in," Mom continued. "He talked me into moving into it. What he didn't tell me was that he owned it. I paid the rent to a real estate company. This is the deed. It's our house now, our very own. And see these…" She was crying as she pulled some more papers from the pouch. "These are U.S. Savings Bonds. Dad took the rent money and put it into bonds for you. They're all made out to you."

Mom turned sideways on the bed and put her hand around the back of my neck. "Do you know what this means?" she asked. It was all happening too suddenly for me to process the facts, much less consider what it could all possibly mean. I'm sure the dazed condition of my mind was plastered across my face. Mom shook my head playfully. "Bud, it means we're set. I already have an offer on this house. With the money from selling this place, and not having to pay rent, we can have enough dough set aside that I can quit that lousy factory and go back to school. I can go to the community college and in a couple of years I can have a real good job with a real future."

Mom had what, under other circumstances, might have been described as a goofy grin on her face. Shaking her head, she murmured, "Dad, Dad, Dad. You were a sly old rascal."

Then she handed me the cigar box again. The final item rattling around inside was a leather tabbed key ring with a couple of keys. I pulled it out of the box and held it up. "What's this for?" I asked.

"Dad's truck."

"What?" I was stunned even more than I already had been. I stood and looked out the rear window. It was all too overwhelming. I was sure I would wake up sometime soon and it would all be a dream--a weird, fascinating, horrible dream.

Mom's voice broke through again. "That Chevy half-ton sitting out in the driveway. It's only a year old. We can park it until you turn sixteen. Then it'll be yours. That's how Dad wanted it. He talked a lot about you there toward the end; about how he wouldn't be here to do things for you. But mostly he talked about how he wouldn't be here to do things with you, and that, maybe, by giving you his truck and watch and stuff that it would almost be like doing things with you."

I turned away from the window and stepped over to where Mom was sitting. We held each other and wept for the love and generosity of the man we would now never be able to thank. Over Mom's shoulder, I saw Robin with bowed head and closed eyes. I wondered if it were possible that Robin was conveying our thanks for us.

Mom squeezed me tight and whispered in my ear, "Happy Birthday, Bud." Then she put her forehead against mine and wiggled her face back and forth, her nose bumping mine, until I started laughing.

We finished packing the things Mom wanted from Grampa's belongings, put them in the car and drove home. When I saw our house, it hit me that for the first time in my life, this could truly be called our home. It wasn't just a house we lived in and could be kicked out of. This was our house. This was our home.

That evening Mom made arrangements with Big Jack for us to be taken back to Grampa's place so that she could drive the truck home. Home; I wondered if I'd ever get tired of the word. Big Jack helped us load a couple of things into the back of the truck. Then, Mom and I got in the cab and brought my truck to my home. She drove down the alley behind the house and parked the beast under the box elder tree next to the storage shed. Jack and Big Jack came over and helped unload the barbeque grill, the new power lawn mower, and the rest of the stuff. Among the items we had brought home was the bicycle I had never learned to ride. That was a condition I was determined to change before school started. I had a week.

CHAPTER THIRTEEN

By Tuesday afternoon, with Jack's help, I had found my center of gravity and was riding that old bike up and down the alley. I had a few scrapes on my elbows and a bruise on my shin where I had fallen against a metal burn barrel. I was glad the people hadn't burned their trash yet that day; the bruise was bad enough without the additional agony of a burn. But every time I had fallen, I had gotten back up and tried again. This was just a mechanical device that millions of others have conquered, I told myself. It does not have a will of its own. It can't out think me. I can do this. I can do this. I can do this. Before you know it…, actually it was the better part of two days to get it done the first time, and a couple of more days to perfect my ability. But the point is, I did it. At no point did I not think I could, I just wasn't sure when. It did help, however, to have Jack there, steadying the bike and cheering me on.

The bicycle was ancient, with big balloon tires and a coaster brake that worked by reversing the pedals, but when I got on that saddle, the wind in my face, I felt like Marlon Brando from "The Wild One" on his big Triumph motorcycle cruising the California coast highway. Jack got out his bike and showed me how to clip a playing card to the frame with a clothespin so that the card hit the turning spokes making a motorcycle sound. Together we roared up the street to the schoolyard.

Jefferson Elementary was a small building and we would be together in the school's only sixth grade class. I told Jack as much as I knew about the teacher we would be sharing, Mrs. Lindsey. I warned him about her reputation for using "the board of education" on unruly students. (Spanking was not only allowed; it was expected.) I described the layout of the building; the gym which doubled as a lunch room, the principal's office, the nurse's office, and most importantly, the location of the boys' restrooms. There were already teachers moving about the building, getting ready for the school year, but we decided against going in. What with Monday being Labor Day, school didn't start until Tuesday, and Tuesday would be soon enough to cross the thresh-hold and leave freedom behind. Mona had already come to the school and formally enrolled Jack and the twins, meeting their teachers and giving the principal copies of Jack's official school records and transcripts.

When Tuesday rolled around, Mom woke me up before she left for work. She gave me a kiss and wished me well. I got up and dressed in the clothes I had worn to Grampa's funeral, all except the tie. It was fake and everybody knew it was fake and if I never wore it again that was all right by me. We had money in the bank now, what with the estate sale, and as soon as the sale of Grampa's house closed, Mom would be quitting that lousy factory and going to school herself. But even having money, Mom hadn't had the chance to get me any other clothes for school yet.

I ate my breakfast, finishing the last of Mom's morning coffee. After all, she had gone beyond the Sunday morning routine by her own choice. My reasoning was that until she told me I couldn't drink coffee, the pot was fair game, especially if she wasn't around to notice. I wouldn't exactly call it rebellion. I thought of it as testing the boundaries of my universe.

I stuffed my book bag with pens, pencils, dictionary and writing tablets. Actually, I was looking forward to school. I had always liked school; it was the other students that I had problems with. I went out to the sidewalk to wait for Jack. Mona had already told Jack that he couldn't ride his bike to school because he had to walk with the twins. So Jack and I strolled up the sidewalk with the twins skipping on ahead.

"I'm gonna need you to show me the ropes," Jack said.

"I'll do what I can," I said. "But I ought to tell you, a lot of kids don't like me."

"Why is that?" Jack asked.

"Well, they think I'm a show-off, 'cause I know so much from reading and stuff."

"Oh," said Jack, a grin splitting his face. "They don't like brainy kids, huh?"

"Not really."

"Good." Jack turned to me, one eye winking behind his hornrims. "We'll show 'em. You and me. Yes-sir-ee Bob. We'll show 'em."

"Are you a brainiac?" I asked.

"I don't talk about it much." Jack said with a wave of his hand, like you see the movie stars do when they don't want their picture taken. "But I've gotten straight A's all my life." Jack wheeled around with a look of real concern. "Don't tell my dad I told you. He doesn't like it when I brag. He says a man's deeds should do the talking for him. The last thing I need is my dad mad at me right now."

Big Jack wasn't called Big Jack for nothing. I wouldn't want him mad at me either. I had heard stories about red hair and fiery tempers, and had no desire to experience it firsthand. But it bugged me that Jack might be afraid of his dad.

"Does your dad hit you?" I asked, fearing the answer.

"Oh, no," Jack said, with a downward shake of his hand. "I can't remember the last time he gave me a swat. He yells sometimes, but, no, he never hits."

"Then what's the problem?"

"It's the restaurant. He and Mona are working their tails off night and day, trying to get this thing open by this week-end and get some coins coming in. He just doesn't need anything else to annoy him. My dad learned his punishment method from one of his Skippers, a guy he calls Captain Beeno. Whenever the guys on the ship would do something wrong, the Skipper would say, 'There will be no movies. There will be no liberty. There will be no card playing.' So, Dad doesn't hit. He says, 'There will be no leaving the house. There will be no TV. There will be no whatever.' Good old Captain Beeno, where ever you are, I hate you."

Jack had such a hang-dog look on his face that I just had to laugh. He looked up with a twinkle in his eye and joined me. I made a key in the lock gesture with my hand on my lips and said, "My lips are sealed."

When we got to the schoolyard, the doors were open and kids were walking into the building. Saying he would have to help "the brats" find their room, Jack took one by each hand and headed through the door. I stood for a moment in the yard, wondering what the year held in store. I was a sixth grader now, one of the supposed kings of the elementary school food chain. I knew already who would rule the playground, who would set the social pecking order during recess, and who would be the last picked in the games. For sheer soul numbing weirdness "The Twilight Zone" couldn't hold a candle to grade school.

The final bell had rung and Mrs. Lindsey was giving out seat assignments when the principal brought Jack to the room door. He whispered in Mrs. Lindsey's ear, nodding toward Jack. After the principal left, Mrs. Lindsey took Jack by the hand, turned to face the class and said, "Boys and girls, this is Jack Anderson. He just transferred here from San Diego, California. Please make him feel welcome." The class clapped and a few of the students said a loud "Hello." I watched her lead Jack to a desk on the opposite side of the room and wave her hand at the empty seat. "Why don't you sit here, Jack?" Rats, I thought. Couldn't she see that there was a perfectly good empty seat right behind me? Oh, well.

The day passed quickly as we received our books and were given our first assignments. As predicted, Mrs. Lindsey told us to write a paper on "How I Spent My Summer Vacation." For a moment, just for a moment, I was tempted to write about my friendship with Robin Hood, but I quickly decided that it would be more than Mrs. Lindsey could probably handle. Instead, I wrote about my grandfather. I wrote about the hospital, and the funeral with the VFW guy and the minister, and I ended the paper writing about the gifts from my grandfather's estate. My conclusion read: "The greatest gift my grandfather gave me this summer was his love. The truck will rust, the watch will lose time, and the knife will dull, but his love will always be mine, living in my heart for the rest of my life." To my embarrassment, after lunch, Mrs. Lindsey chose my essay to read to the rest of the class. When she finished all the other kids were looking at me. "Oh, great," I said to myself. "This is not a fine start." I could see Jack on the other side of the room, smiling and nodding his head.

As we were walking home, Jack said, "Man, I wish I could write like that."

"What do you mean?" I asked.

"What do I mean? What do you mean, what do I mean? Cat, you had 'em. You hooked 'em. You had your head down. You weren't watching. I was watching, and, man, they were eating it up."

"Yeah, right." Running through my mind was: "Eating it up my eye! They were just looking for another excuse to think I was goofy. They don't like me. How can they like what I write?" It's amazing the things you will believe simply because it's your own brain telling you.

Punching me lightly on the shoulder, Jack said, "No, man, come on. It was great. Give yourself some credit." Stopping at the corner, Jack turned and nailed me out of left field. "Maybe they don't like you because you don't let them. It's like you would rather be in a cave, playing Robinson Crusoe or something."

How dare he pass judgment on me? Angrily I snarled, "And what does that make you? Friday?"

Jack's ears were flaming as he barked back, "Don't get huffy with me."

"What?" I yelled. "You think I need you? I don't need you!. I don't need anybody!"

I fled down the street, on the verge of tears, leaving Jack to follow along herding the twins.

I don't know what happened. If only the teacher had not read my essay. So what if I could write. It's my writing. It's a part of me. It's personal and maybe I don't want to get that personal with anybody. Maybe I like my cave. Was I in a cave? Was I hiding from people who weren't attacking? He was only paying me a compliment. Can I write? My head was reeling. I felt like John Henry had picked up his nine-pound hammer and was punching his tunnel through right behind my eyes. I needed to run. I needed to escape. I needed to somehow just get away. My rescuer came disguised as a large wooden box with a black and white picture tube.

I was watching a "Jungle Jim" episode on Cap'n Bob's Riverboat when I heard a knock at the front door. Through the screen I could see Jack standing on the porch. I walked over and stood with the screen door between us. Jack cocked his head to one side and shrugged his shoulders. "I'm really sorry, man," he said. "Can I talk to you?"

No, my mind yelled. Go away! I hate you! You're one of them.

Instead, I stepped out onto the porch, holding the screen door open in case I needed a quick escape. "It's your nickel," I said, my voice bitter and cold.

When I looked Jack in the face, I was surprised to see that his eyes were sad and red-rimmed and wet. Jack crying? I couldn't believe it. Why would Jack be crying?

"Maybe it's true. Maybe you don't need me." Jack's voice was real low, not quite a whisper. "But I need you. I need somebody."

I stepped away from the door, letting it slam shut. "Why?' I asked.

"I didn't have any friends back in San Diego," Jack said. "Do you know what it's like to have a new bunch of people moving in and out of your life every six months? On a Navy base kids are always moving away. Just when you're getting to like somebody, to know somebody, they're gone. I'm tired of starting all over again." Jack waved his arms out by his sides. "I can laugh and joke and talk to people about things that don't really matter down deep inside, but I don't have a clue how to make friends. I don't know. I thought that maybe, seeing that neither of us are gonna be moving in six months, I thought that maybe you might be a friend

I could have for a long time." He dropped his hands to his sides and rubbed his sneaker toe against the porch floorboards. "Does it have to be this way?"

Relief flooded up in me in a way that I'd never experienced before. Rubbing my hand across my bristled head, I said, "I'm not very good at this being friends business. I don't know how it works. But I'm willing to bury the hatchet if you are, just so it's not in each other's back."

"Then can we start again?"

"Sure," I said, a grin starting to work its way across my face. "Do you like 'Jungle Jim'?"

"Does a cat like cream?" Jack said with a smile.

"Then come on in, time's a 'wasting."

CHAPTER FOURTEEN

It was two weeks into the school year. Big Jack and Mona had their place open and it was a hit. They served pizza, which was a new experience for the town. People came from all over the county for one of Big Jack's pies. He even had boxes so somebody could call up and have a pizza ready to take home. Mom and I had been down a couple of times, and I must confess that pizza soon became one of my all-time favorite foods. Jack was busy every week-end and Big Jack told me that I could have a job in a couple of years if Mom would sign the work papers.

One afternoon I left Jefferson Elementary wondering how to convert Jack to the Cubs. When it came to baseball, all he wanted to talk about was the New York Yankees. Jack seemed to think moonbeams twinkled out of Mickey Mantle's behind. Jack and I had spent so much time together that it felt odd to be walking home alone. Mona had taken him and the twins to the eye-doctor as soon as school let out for the day.

As I neared our house, I heard the sound of Robin's silver horn coming from the direction of "Sherwood Forest." I hadn't exactly been avoiding Robin, but I hadn't seen much of him lately either. I zoomed into the house, threw my book-bag on the sofa and headed to my room to change out of my school clothes. Moments later, dressed in ratty sneakers, cut-off jeans and my favorite well-worn Cubs t-shirt, I was trotting down the street. I leaped the culvert bordering the road and slid through the gap in the bushes on the edge of the grove. I was looking forward to seeing my friend once again. Until I had heard his horn, I hadn't realized just how much I missed Robin of the Hood.

Robin was leaning against the tree where we had first met. "How are you, my young scholar? Are you applying yourself?" There was a smile on his face and a twinkle in his eyes.

"Well," I said. "I'm trying to not be the first to raise my hand, to let other kids have a chance. I don't always remember, but I'm trying."

"Does it help to have competition?" Robin asked.

"What do you mean?" Duh. Not my brightest response.

"The other boy in your class, the new boy. The one who may be as bright as you, if not brighter."

Tilting my head, I said, "Do you know about Jack?"

Robin put a who-are-you-kidding look on his face. "Yes," Robin said slowly. "Even though you have not gotten around to introducing us, I know about Jack."

"Does it bother you that I haven't brought Jack down here?" I asked.

"No," Robin said, shaking his head. "It doesn't bother me. You will bring him down here someday."

"I don't know if I can," I said softly, looking down at the creek.

"Why?" Robin's voice was just as soft.

Why? The question to end all questions. The question that drives mothers of two-year-olds half-crazy. Why? Why, indeed? Or, better yet, why not?

Rubbing my face with my hand, I turned to look into Robin's eyes. "It's all so hard. I mean, how do I explain you? You lived eight hundred years ago." Waving my hand around at the trees, I continued. "This isn't really Sherwood Forest and I don't live in Nottingham. It's all so crazy." Dropping my hands to my sides, my shoulders sagging, I faced the truth head on. "I don't want him to think I'm nuts."

The sun was low enough that the light hit Robin's eyes in such a way that they gleamed as if with a life of their own. "What is madness?" he said. "The inability to dream, the unwillingness to dream, the denial of dreaming—that is madness. The refusal to chase dreams—that is madness. To be unaccepting of an active imagination—that is madness. To have as reality only that which one can put in one's purse—that is the ultimate madness. You are not mad, my young friend. In a world gone mad, you have shown yourself to be caring and brave and faithful. A bit on the withdrawn side, perhaps, but mad?—No, dear one, you are not mad."

I stood up straight and noticed that as I looked into Robin's face, I didn't have to tilt my head as much as before. Either Robin had shrunk, or I had grown. I wasn't sure which.

"I still don't know how to explain you," I said sadly.

Robin looked away this time. "You won't have to explain anything. He will never meet me. I won't be here."

He should have just shot me with an arrow. The pain in my heart would have been less. "What?" I cried. "You're leaving? You can't leave."

Robin turned back to me with a smile, a smile that didn't quite reach his eyes. "Remember when we met? Remember what I told you? 'An ally to the oppressed, bringing aid to those in need.' You have been a dear, true friend, but…"

"But what? I'm never gonna see you again?"

"You no longer need me. There are others who do."

"What's that supposed to mean?" My head was spinning. I felt angry and betrayed.

Standing upright, his hands clasped on the top of his longbow, Robin said, "You were a friendless lad who had erected a fortress out of books and movies. Due to conditions not all of your own making, you were afraid to allow anyone else to cross the moat and enter the fortress. You are not afraid any longer. You have let one person in. He will not be the last."

"But, why do you have to go?" I moaned.

"Do you think you are the only young person who has constructed such a fortress? Others need my help, and I must go."

Breathing a sigh of resignation, I said, "I won't ever see you again will I?"

Robin smiled, the smile reaching his eyes this time. "Oh, I don't know. As your first friend, you might see glimpses of me in the faces of the friends yet to come."

I looked down at my shoes. "I'll never forget you," I said. "I owe you so much. I love you, Robin."

When I looked up I found that I had been speaking to the trees and the creek.

Robin of the Hood was gone.

GARY WELLS

CHAPTER FIFTEEN

I'm in my fifties now. I still read books. I still watch movies. I still root for the Chicago Cubs. I drink a lot of coffee, although I smooth it out with flavored creamer. I still listen to the radio. I even worked as a disc jockey for a few years. Wheaties is still my breakfast cereal of choice and pizza is a regular part of my diet. But most of all, I still make friends. As a matter of fact, my friends are an extremely important part of my identity. Friendship has never been without pain; the allowing of people past my defense mechanisms is still not an easy thing for me. I don't know if pain helps, hinders, or has no effect at all on the maturing process. What I do know is that the things that haven't come easy have the most value. My friends have an extreme amount of value.

I didn't grow up that summer. I had other internal battles to fight, other victories to embrace, other horizons to conquer. But finding out that I had what it took to be a man—a real man, not just an aging adolescent—was a major step in the direction of growing up.

Eventually I did grow up. I traveled to far off places, saw some amazing sights, and did some outstanding things. I married and had children, children that I introduced to Captain Blood and Tarzan and a host of other heroes from my childhood. I learned more about taxes than I cared to know. I have continued to write while living a life that has contained something about which to write. I am not a spectator. I am the home team. I have learned that there are things that, no matter how hard I try, I cannot do. But those are lessons I learned by trying, not by refusing to try.

I never saw Robin again. But all through these years, sometimes, just sometimes, when I found myself up against something I felt was beyond my ability to handle, I would hear, faintly on the breeze, a silver hunting horn, and I would know, down deep where all true knowing takes place, that help was near and I was safe.

THE END

BONUS STORIES

GARY WELLS

A HELL OF A NOTE

I woke up in a box. My heart was beating like a trip-hammer and there was a tingling, kind of like electricity, running throughout my body. I had feeling in my arms and legs but I couldn't move them. I tried blinking my eyes, not knowing whether I was blind or just in a dark place.

The last thing I could remember was playing my favorite, well-used Fender Stratocaster on a cramped stage in a crowded, smoky bar. Some bonehead drunk had spilled a pitcher of beer on my amplifier and a bright blue light had streaked up my guitar cord. From then on everything was blank.

"Am I dead?" I thought. "Is this a coffin?"

But I couldn't be dead. I still had feeling. I still had memory. I still had a pulse. I also still had hearing. I realized that when I noticed a couple of metallic clicks off to my right. And I wasn't blind. A line of light appeared, also to my right. Then there was a lot of light as the box lid, apparently hinged on my left, was lifted.

A face loomed over me, looking me up and down. "Help me," I tried to yell. I tried, but no sound came out.

Then a hand reached down, grabbed me behind the neck and lifted me out of the box; lifted me with one hand as if I weighed next to nothing. To add to my amazement, I didn't bend. It was as if a steel rod ran from the back of my head down to my toes. The guy laid me on a bench of some sort. He brushed his fingers across my chest hair.

"What are you, some kind of pervert? Stop that." At least those were the words in my mind. What came out of my throat was just some gibberish tones.

Then he laid me across his lap and while plucking at my chest hair, began tapping his fingers on my neck. I heard myself uttering more gibberish. Then he started twisting my ears while playing with my chest hair. "This has got to be some kind of psychotic dream," I thought. I tried moving, but it was as if I were made of wood. There was no wiggle to me at all.

Then, holding me by the neck, the guy carried me to a large window, like a storefront display window. He propped me up facing the glass. Outside the window I could see a busy street. The store, or whatever it was, must have been at an intersection because every so often traffic would stop and a line of cars would form. Then the cars would move the way they would if a light had turned green.

While I was propped there in the window, a spikey-haired kid with a studded dog collar and a t-shirt from some hard-rock band stopped and looked in at me. Putting his nose to the glass, he cupped his hands around his face to shade his eyes. He put his lips together like he was whistling. Then with a shrug of his shoulders he turned and was gone.

"Has the whole world gone crazy?" I said to myself. "Or is it just me?"

The traffic began slowing down again and I saw the front of a delivery truck come into view. On the side of the truck door I read, 'Acme Glass and Mirrors.' When the truck was fully stopped, I was looking at a large wall-sized mirror. In the reflection of the mirror I saw the store window. Reading the print in reverse, I saw the words 'Pawn Shop.' Alone in the pawn shop window was a battered electric guitar; a well-used Fender Stratocaster.

THE END

THE BOY NEXT DOOR

My daughter looked so regal, so lovely, as we stood arm in arm at the main entrance to the church sanctuary. Through mist-covered eyes I could almost see Billy, up front, by the altar rail. My mind went back to when Billy and his family had moved in next door to us. He had been five at the time. My daughter, Jessica, had been three.

Over the years, our families did a lot of things together. We had barbeques and camping trips and Super Bowl Parties. We dug each others' cars out of the snow every winter, shared a rented roto-tiller every spring, and kept an eye on each others' houses when the other family would go on vacation. Tom, Billy's Dad, helped me re-shingle my roof after the big wind of '97. I helped them clean up their basement when a water pipe burst and flooded the rec room.

But mostly, we watched our children grow up together.

Jessica pitched a fit when she found out that Billy was going to be riding a bus across town to the Middle School while she still had two years at the elementary school down at the end of the street.

"It isn't fair," she ranted. "We been walking to school together all my life."

"He's two years older than you," I said, quite reasonably, I thought.

"So. That's not my fault."

When Billy was in High School, and got his driver's license, he offered to give Jess a ride to and from school every day. It was not a suggestion that I looked upon with much favor.

"He's a nice boy," my wife told me.

"Yeah, a nice kid whose sap is rising in the tree."

"They're good kids. You have to learn to trust them."

"I trust them to be teen-agers who haven't got a clue. I don't trust them to be mature and in control of their emotions and impulses."

That summer I moved my weight set out under a canopy in the back yard. I let Billy see me doing fifty pound dumbbell curls.

When Billy was seventeen, he asked Jessica to go to the Junior Prom. I led Billy into the back yard for a chat. I stared across my weight bench at him.

"Mister," I told him. "That little girl is one of the few things I value more than my own life. You get out of line with her and I will give you good reason to welcome death. You understand me?"

I'll give him this. He stood on his hind legs like a man and looked me straight in the eye. "Sir," he said. "My parents raised me better than you think. Jessica means a lot to me, and I think, I hope, I mean a lot to her. I would never do anything to betray that."

"OK," I said. "But remember this, nothing good happens after midnight. I'll be waiting up."

That night I was sitting in my easy chair when Billy brought Jessica to the door. After they said their good-byes, she turned to me in anger.

"Why do you hate him so much?"

Putting my crossword puzzle book down, I looked at her. "I don't hate him," I said.

"But you don't trust him."

"No, I don't. I trust him more than I do any other guy, otherwise I wouldn't have let you go with him. But, do I trust him completely? No, I don't."

"Are you trying to drive him away?"

"If I can."

"But, Whyyyyyy?" she wailed.

"Because," I said quite firmly. "If his desire and affection for you is not greater than his fear of me, he does not deserve you. I will do anything and everything I can, short of beating the crap out of him, to run him off. If I can't, then more power to him. But, if I can, then I will."

"But, what if I love him?"

"It doesn't matter. What matters is does he love you. If he doesn't, then he's history and good riddance."

My daughter didn't talk to me for a while after that. It was a lonely time.

A few years went by.

Billy got a job working construction in the summers and going to the University in the off-season, studying pre-law. Jessica went to classes at the U and got a job working in a bookstore evenings and weekends. For fiscal reasons, they both continued living at home. They studied together in my living room. They dated, with Billy continuing to make sure Jess was in the front door by midnight.

It was shortly after his graduation when Billy, Bill by now, asked me if he could marry my daughter. I didn't make it easy for him, but I finally did say that it was OK with me. But before any plans could be firmed up, The United States of America was attacked. I'm sure you remember where you were when you heard about the Twin Towers, and the Pentagon, and the plane that went down in Pennsylvania. Bill and Jessica sat out on his parents' back stoop for hours that evening. The following afternoon Bill came over and told me that as much as he loved my daughter, he felt honor-bound to respond to his country's need. He told me that he had enlisted earlier that day and that he and Jessica had agreed to postpone the wedding until his military service time was over. I took him by the hand and told him I was proud that I was going to have him in my family.

Now, with my daughter clinging to my arm, I begin walking down the aisle. The pews are full and soft music is playing. On the very edge of my senses, I notice an occasional whisper. I can imagine what's being said about Jessica and the boy next door, the boy who continued to love my daughter despite my best efforts to run him off, the boy who became the man who stood tall when he was needed, the man whose body now lies in the coffin at the end of the aisle.

I weep.

THE END

THE GUIDE DOG

I awoke with a squishy spot on the side of my head. The phrase "subdural hematoma" came to mind, but I wouldn't want to wager on its accuracy. I knew who I was, but not where I was or how I got there. Apparently the most recent items on my short term memory shelf had gotten jarred loose. What I did know was that I was high up on the side of a mountain, injured and all alone, and a storm was coming on. It was daylight, sort of, what with the dark clouds and all, but I had no idea whether it was morning, afternoon or what.

When I tried to stand, I discovered that my right knee was banged up and didn't want to work properly. Using some cracks on the cliff face I managed to pull myself erect, but oh was my head throbbing by the time I finally got vertical. I was on a little shelf with no sign of a trail leading up or down. The idea came to me that I had been with some other people, but if that were the case, they were long gone. Also long gone was my watch, my wallet and everything else that should have been in my pockets. Had I been with friends? If so, why had they abandoned me high up in the mountains with a storm brewing? Had I been robbed on a mountain road, rolled over the edge of the cliff and left for dead? I didn't have any answers and it hurt my head to think.

It also hurt my eyes to look at things. I seemed to recall that I wore glasses and anything beyond two feet became a progressive blur. If memory served me correctly it was called being near-sighted.

The wind was started to howl and icy snow began flicking my cheek. "Oh, man," I thought. "What am I going to do?" I looked heaven-ward. "Lord, I could sure use some help right about now," I prayed. Then I slid into a sitting position, my aching back pressed against the rocky mountainside. I was so tired, so tired, so tired.

I was awaked by a dog's snout snuffling my ear.

"Wha…?"

I turned and looked into the deep brown eyes of the most gorgeous Golden Retriever I had ever seen. I knew all about Golden Retrievers. I had one when I was a boy. I had called her "Maple" because her coat was that rich light brown of maple syrup, like liquid gold. I had always thought Golden Retrievers to be the most loyal, most noble breed of dog that God had put on this planet. Maple had died in a boating accident when I was ten. She had rescued me but at the cost of her own life. I never got a replacement.

I reached out and rubbed the dog's fur where the neck blends into the shoulder. She leaned up against me, her tongue out and panting in that "Ooh, do that some more" way that dogs have.

"Where did you come from, girl?" I asked. I didn't verify the gender; force of habit led me to refer to the dog in feminine terms.

The dog sat back on her hind haunches, cocked her head to one side, and then with a yip looked down the side of the mountain. Then she looked back at me and yipped again.

"Down there? You came from down there?" I asked.

She yipped.

"This is goofy," I said. "Here I am, on the side of a mountain having a conversation with a mystery dog."

She yipped again.

"Do you understand what I'm saying?"

The dog leaped to her feet and yipped twice.

"Then you need to go get somebody. Tell them Timmy fell up the well."

The dog lay down with her front paws pointed toward me.

"What? Is it just you and me? Is that what you're trying to tell me?"

She cocked her to one side again and yipped.

"Well, I can't walk. So what do we do about that?"

She jumped to her feet and disappeared over the side of the cliff, don't ask me how. After all, I hadn't seen a trail. On the other hand I was nearly blind without my glasses.

In less time than it takes to tell, she was back with a small tree branch in her mouth. It was about an inch thick and three feet long. The end that had been attached to the tree was large and rounded like a knob. It was the perfect walking stick. She dropped the branch next to my leg and pushed her nose under my elbow.

I looped my arm behind her neck and rubbed the top of her head between her ears. Her tongue came out and her chest went up and down, enjoying the attention. "I guess you are a retriever after all, aren't you, girl?" I tilted my weary head and looked at the sky. Even with my bad eyes I could tell it was getting darker and the clouds were dancing around like water at full boil. The snow was getting heavier and starting to drift up against my pantsleg.

The dog, (I was starting to think of her as "Maple, Junior) pushed against the stick with her nose, knocking the knob into my hand. "Well, Mapes," I said, with more enthusiasm than I really felt. "Are you telling me it's time to travel on?" I reached up and got a handhold in a crack of the rock face. Balancing myself with the stick, I levered myself upright, gasping for breath by the time I got to my feet.

"OK, pup," I panted. "What now?"

Maple, Junior went to one side of the ledge, looked over her shoulder at me, and yipped. I hobbled over, using the stick to take as much weight as possible off my bad knee. When I got up beside the dog, lo and behold, there was a trail weaving down through the rocks. I couldn't see it very well past the first few feet, but at least I knew where to safely put my first step, and the step after that, and the step after that. One step at a time.

I don't know how far we traveled, it seemed like miles, or how long it took, it seemed like ages, but with every step the dog was there. She nudged me when I stopped, braced me when I started to slip, and in general, herded me like a lost little lamb.

Finally, we came around a bend in the rocks and spread out before us was a beautiful sunlit valley. Even with my bad eyesight I could see a river in the distance with lush trees growing along the far side. The grass was green, like those pictures you see of Ireland. There was a flock of sheep, with a shepherd in attendance, near the river.

Holding on to the staff, I leaned over and scratched the dog between the eyes. "Is that your flock, girl?" I said. "Is that your master?" The dog shook herself with a joyous wiggle. Then she nudged my thigh with her shoulder as if to say, "Let's get a move on."

As soon as my foot left the rocky path and touched the grass the really weird stuff started. First off, my pain left; my leg, my head, my back, it was all gone. Then I noticed, wonder of wonders, that I could see. The dog leaped up with a happy yip and put her paws on my chest. I dropped the stick and started rubbing my thumbs against her ribs. "Good dog. Good dog," I said in a sing-songy voice. I cocked my head to one side. "Man, you sure look like Maple."

She dropped down and rubbed her neck against my leg. I reached down and turned her collar tags up the light. Dangling from the buckle was a small brass tag stamped with the word "Maple." I jumped back. "But, you died when I was ten. How can you be Maple?" The dog turned her head and looked back up the way we had come.

I also turned, and with my new eagle-eye vision, saw, high on a rocky ledge, a snow covered body; my body. From behind me I heard, "Well done, good and faithful servant. Enter into your Master's rest."

THE END

ABOUT THE AUTHOR

If you look out the corner of your eye at a fun-house mirror reflection of the boy in the story you will see glimpses of the author.

A life-long Cubs fan, who still has a crush on Maureen O'Hara, Mr. Wells did ask for Wheaties when his tonsils were removed, got locked in the library after hours, and spent many a summer afternoon under a shade tree reading books.

Mr. Wells wrote Sports for a local weekly while in high school, did movie reviews and wrote an opinion column for his collage paper, and worked almost a decade as a radio disc jockey.

He has collected a drawer full of blue ribbons over the years from the Creative Writing division of his state fair. The Silver Horn of Robin Hood is his first novel.

www.ingramcontent.com/pod-product-compliance
Lightning Source LLC
Chambersburg PA
CBHW021154020426
42331CB00003B/60